CONTENTS

List of Tables		6
List of Figures		6
Chapter 1	Introduction	7
Chapter 2	An Historical Note	21
Chapter 3	Define or Be Defined!	25
Chapter 4	Official Statistics on Prevalence and Cost	35
Chapter 5	Of Motives and Meanings	47
Chapter 6	Graffiti - Urban Scourge or Folk Art?	61
Chapter 7	Attacks on Defensible Space	69
Chapter 8	To Blazes with School!	77
Chapter 9	Prevention	85
Chapter 10	Recommendations	99
Appendix	Sources of Practical Help	117
Bibliography		119

LIST OF TABLES

Table 1.1	The prevalence of vandalism	13
Table 4.1	Criminal damage per 100,000 population by area	38
Table 5.1	Percentage choosing as very important causes of vandalism	58

LIST OF FIGURES

Figure 4.1	Notifiable offences in England and Wales 1950-1989	36
Figure 4.2	Persons found guilty of, or cautioned for, indictable offences by offence group and age	39
Figure 4.3	Levels of recorded and unrecorded crime, 1987	42
Figure 4.4	The rising price of vandalism to schools	45
Figure 4.5	Total cost of school vandalism adjusted for inflation	45
Figure 5.1	Percentage of respondents admitting to having been a vandal	50
Figure 5.2	Explanations of vandalism	60

Vandalism

& Graffiti

The state of the art

Frank Coffield

Calouste Gulbenkian Foundation,
London, 1991

DEDICATION

To Mary, Emma and Thomas as a small recompense for the time spent away from them on this report;

and to Stan Cohen who continues to ask the right questions.

ACKNOWLEDGEMENTS

Ben Whitaker, Director of the Gulbenkian Foundation, encouraged me from the first moment to the last and I want publicly to acknowledge his support. My friends Peter Rogers and Jackson Hall took the trouble to read and criticise the manuscript and the final version has been improved by their comments. Dennis Pollard, Research Officer, Northumbria Police kindly gave me permission to quote from his report as did Bloodaxe Books for the three verses from Tony Harrison's poem *V*.

I am also grateful to the Newcastle Chronicle and Journal Limited for allowing me access to their Picture Library and for permission to reproduce some of their pictures on vandalism in this report. Judy Hillman and Bob Bird also read the report and I was happy to receive their comments.

BIOGRAPHICAL NOTE

Frank Coffield is Professor of Education in the School of Education at the University of Durham. After leaving Glasgow University he taught in a Comprehensive School, an Approved School, and Jordanhill College of Education and was Senior Lecturer in Education at Keele University. He is author of several books including *A Glasgow Gang Observed* (Eyre Methuen, 1973); *A Cycle of Deprivation?* with P Robinson and J Sarsby (Heinemann, 1980); *Sacred Cows in Education* edited with Richard Goodings (Edinburgh University Press, 1983); and *Growing up at the Margins: Young Adults in the North East* (Open University Press, 1986) with C Borrill and S Marshall. His most recent title, *Risky Business? Youth and the Enterprise Culture*, written with Dr R MacDonald (Falmer Press, 1991), he is extending into a study of the changing cultures of work in the North East.

CHAPTER 1

INTRODUCTION

Let me guess that the reader who has just opened this report on vandalism is hoping that the following questions will be satisfactorily answered in subsequent pages: Why is so much property deliberately defaced or maliciously destroyed? Is the problem getting worse? What are the financial and social costs? Why are some countries like Sweden or Switzerland less vandalised than Britain, France or the States? Is the problem largely confined to certain types of area (for example, run-down, inner urban estates), and specific kinds of property (public rather than private)? Must we, as a society, just grin and bear it, as parents are often advised when their children become adolescents, or can it be prevented? And if so, how? Is there an identifiable sub-group of young people whose mindless, wanton and irrational defacement of public property allows them to be identified, charged and treated as vandals? Is their behaviour really 'mindless', 'wanton' and 'irrational'? Are these the most important questions to ask? What insights and suggestions can research offer us?

From the time I was invited to write this report in March 1990, I have increasingly immersed myself in the literature on vandalism, which has turned out to be a much larger body of work than my first computer searches had led me to believe. I only stopped reading when I repeatedly came across factual information and arguments which had become as familiar to me as my children's voices. And to prevent expectations being raised to an unrealistically high level, it may be advisable to set down right at the beginning some of the main conclusions that I have come to after my long 'soak' in the literature.

First, **there is no one theory which has unlocked the secrets of vandalism**. Instead, there are a number of competing approaches or schools of thought, each of which tends to explain, in my view, only part of the problem or just one particular type of vandalism. As we shall see, there is no agreement about the definition, scale or seriousness of the problem; there are no generally recognised means of recording data so that measurement and estimates of cost vary from report to report. In consequence, it is impossible to state whether vandalism is on the increase or diminishing in this country nor can meaningful comparisons be made between investigations carried out here with studies completed in other countries. It is also a matter of personal preference to decide which conditions foster or prevent its occurrence because commentators are quite clearly studying different types of vandalism. In short, too many studies of vandalism tend to be theoretically weak; they are bedevilled by problems of definition, and they do not build on previous work.

But if theoretical ideas and cumulative research reports are thin on the ground, the very opposite is true with regard to strategies for prevention. The trouble here is that the <u>quality</u> of the suggestions made is in inverse proportion to their quantity; I collected roughly five times as much material on solutions to, than explanations of, vandalism. The latter involve entering a complex and ambiguous world where ideas clash and ideological positions are never far from the surface. As a result, many commentators tend to ignore (or assume general agreement over) causation and motivation and proceed to discuss their favourite solution(s). But there is, in fact, no magic wand to make the graffiti written by magic markers disappear overnight or, more importantly, to stop the graffiti writers from wanting to 'piece' buildings. The same well-intentioned proposals, which are always couched in the most optimistic of terms, tend to be strongly advocated at conference after conference on reducing vandalism, but one listens in vain for convincing evidence of their effectiveness. Conviction without evaluation tends to be the order of the day at such meetings.

Sperandio (1984, p 105), in an article interestingly entitled 'Vandalism as a Fact of Life in Society', accurately sums up the current state of our knowledge: "At the present time it is probably premature to seek a single explanatory system..."; the data are so contradictory and "...fragmentary that they tend to lead to questions rather than solutions". **So readers should be warned: we have so far developed neither a comprehensive theory to explain vandalism nor a single, successful strategy to prevent it.** There are, however, a number of indications in the literature which suggest positive ways forward.

Most of the commentators tend to strike moral poses and their writing is dull, repetitive and predictable stuff. Chief constables, for example, apparently unaffected by the research on vandalism and graffiti, seem unable to address a conference on these topics without using the words "senseless", "mindless" and "obscene" (see, for example, Oxford, 1988). Every so often, however, I came across nuggets of gold among the surrounding dross and, even more rarely, a genuine surprise.

The literature does, however, also contain a series of contributions from one sociologist whose writings have transformed the study of vandalism. More than any other author who has studied this topic, Stan Cohen has for almost thirty years brought a freshness of approach and has asked (and continues to ask) a new and intriguing set of questions about vandalism which are as relevant now as when he first posed them. But he has done more than that; he has imposed some order on the field by, for example, suggesting a typology both of vandalism and of methods of control and prevention. Although these classifications were first produced in 1973 they have still, in my opinion, not been improved upon. I wish to acknowledge the continuing importance of Stan Cohen's contribution to the debate, a contribution which began when he set out to dispel two central stereotypes about vandalism, namely, that it is homogeneous and meaningless.

I shall turn to his arguments in a moment but let us begin with one or two surprises. **How many people, for example, know that in England and Wales no-one has ever been charged or found guilty of vandalism, whereas in Scotland since 1980 vandalism has been a criminal offence?** Under the Criminal Justice (Scotland) Act of 1980 (Section 78), which was introduced to avoid the difficulty of proving <u>malicious</u> damage; "...any person who, without reasonable excuse, wifully or recklessly destroys or damages any property belonging to another shall be guilty of the offence of vandalism". In contrast, in England and Wales there is no statutory offence of vandalism, but Section 1 of the Criminal Damage Act of 1971, which talks of "A person who without lawful excuse destroys or damages any property...", covers the type of deliberate destruction or damage which most people refer to as vandalism. The phrase used in *Criminal Statistics, England and Wales 1989* is, again, "criminal damage". This difference in legal approach and terminology has not been quoted as a quaint, abstruse and perhaps mildly interesting piece of knowledge but to make a substantive point, namely, that deviance is a social process which is defined differently even within Great Britain. In other words, what is considered deviant behaviour is neither universally agreed nor an objective, absolute fact of life, but tends to vary both geographically and historically as the citizens of Berwick-upon-Tweed no doubt realise because, over a wide range of offences, it will make considerable differences to them whether they are arrested by Scottish or English police officers.

Second, **how many readers have thought of vandalism as a *solution* rather than a *problem*;** a solution to the difficulties experienced by urban, working-class adolescents growing up in working-class cities? In Stan Cohen's own words (1984a, p 57) "The argument...is that vandalism as a solution to this group's problem is just 'right', both in symbolic, expressive (or emotional) and instrumental terms. That is, in its very senselessness, it makes sense...in terms of what it offers to this group (excitement, trouble, toughness, action, control, taking risks)..."

Indeed, in his earliest writings on the subject (eg 1964), Cohen was one of the first to oppose the notion which is still prevalent that all vandalism can be appropriately described and dismissed as meaningless, irrational and wanton damage. His aim has been to defend the meaning which people give for their actions and to appreciate - without romanticising their plight - the explanations they provide. But why are the accounts, which young people or deviants more generally give of their behaviour, not listened to? Cohen (1971, p 19) replies that:

> *People cannot allow deviation to threaten their picture of what their society is about. Part of this picture involves recognising and accrediting certain motives as legitimate; if these motives cannot be found, then the behaviour cannot be tolerated, it must be neutralised or annihilated. Thus vandalism, unlike theft, cannot be explained in terms of the accredited motive of acquiring material gain, so it is described as motiveless. The only way of making sense of some actions is to assume that they do not make sense. Any other assumption would be threatening. We are very much concerned...with restoring meaning to behaviour which has been stripped of it in this way.*

Third, how are we to respond to the growing numbers of young people who, when questioned about graffiti, respond by saying that they love Hip-Hop art? Witness the 14 year-old girl in Pollard's (1988, p 56) study in the Blyth valley of Northumberland of young people's attitudes to vandalism: "Sometimes vandalism looks nice when breakdancers do colourful things under underpasses, at Metro stations, railway stations etc". Allen (1984, p 82) has summed up the point neatly: "...graffiti can be viewed as art - and as an improvement over the original environment in many cases".

Fourth, the definition of vandalism can be extended to include what David Downes (1974, p 207) has called "pinstripe vandalism", which refers to those vandals who have power "...planners and developers who have damaged our cities and landscapes a thousand times more permanently and irreversibly than all the vandals without power rolled into one".

These issues will all be explored in more detail in later chapters and they have been touched upon here to illustrate a point which will occur again and again: **to study or write about vandalism is to plunge into intellectual uncertainty and political controversy**. What the reader needs who may be coming fresh to these disputes is some framework to help him or her place the various contributions or strands of thought in some historical and epistemological order.

There are four main explanations which have been offered over the years and these can be briefly (but crudely) identified as: the psychological, the sociological, and the architectural to which has recently been added a new approach which emphasises the relationship between individuals and their environment and which talks of a 'socio-environmental system'. (Levy-Leboyer, 1984, was the first to suggest an evolution of four hypotheses concerning vandalism.) Each of these four positions will now be concisely introduced.

Psychologists and psychiatrists have traditionally explained 'senseless' or 'pointless' vandalism by claiming that the offenders are mentally and/or emotionally disturbed and suffer from inherited or acquired personality disorders of one kind or another which necessitate treatment. Conclusions tended to be drawn from intensive, longitudinal studies (eg West, 1969 and 1973a; West and Farrington, 1977) of individuals and their families, which set out to demonstrate that young vandals and, more generally, juvenile delinquents are different in a number of important aspects from their non-delinquent contemporaries.

D J West (1973b, p 466), for instance, concluded that his Cambridge Study in Delinquent Development "...confirmed that delinquents do in fact differ from, and are in many ways inferior to or less fortunate than, their non-delinquent school fellows". But the attempt to label all young vandals disturbed or maladjusted came seriously unstuck when researchers began to conduct 'self-report' studies, where, for example, representative samples of adolescent boys were asked to confess to the extent of their involvement in a range of destructive behaviours. F J Gladstone (1978, p 23) studied almost 600 boys aged 11 to 15 attending secondary schools in a northern city in England in 1973, and his findings about the prevalence of vandalism are presented in Table 1.1. He drew the following conclusions:

Table 1.1

The prevalence of vandalism

1.	Scratched desk at school	85%
2.	Broken a bottle in the street	79%
3.	Broken a window in an empty house	68%
4.	Written on walls in the street	65%
5.	Broken trees or flowers in a park	58%
6.	Written on the seats or walls of buses	55%
7.	Broken the glass in a street lamp	48%
8.	Scratched a car or lorry	42%
9.	Smashed things on a building site	40%
10.	Broken a window in an occupied house	32%
11.	Broken the glass in a bus shelter	32%
12.	Damaged park building	31%
13.	Broken furniture at school	29%
14.	Broken a window in a public toilet	29%
15.	Broken the glass of a telephone kiosk	28%
16.	Broken a car radio aerial	28%
17.	Damaged the tyres of a car	28%
18.	Broken a window at school	27%
19.	Slashed bus seats	22%
20.	Broken a seat in a public toilet	20%
21.	Damaged telephone in a kiosk	20%
22.	Put large objects on a railway line	19%
23.	Broken a window in a club	16%
24.	Slashed train seats	12%

Percentages refer to the proportion of boys who admitted to having committed the specified act at least once in the previous six months.

Source: Gladstone, F J (1978) 'Vandalism among Adolescent Schoolboys', p 23

It would appear that such acts as breaking a bottle in the street or a window in an empty house are so common as to be more or less normal behaviour, at least in the city where the study took place. And if such acts are counted as vandalism then nearly all the boys were 'vandals'. Most of the destructive behaviour involved only a minority of the boys, however, so that although it is important to recognise that between the occasional bottle smasher and the persistent wrecker lies a continuum of involvement rather than a moral gulf, there is none the less

reasonable ground for making some sort of distinction between 'petty' and
'serious' vandalism even if any cut-off point is bound to be somewhat arbitrary.

Sociologists also began to challenge the dominance of the classical psychological approach by arguing that acts of criminal damage tend to be committed by groups rather than by individuals acting on their own. They also contended that the traditional emphasis on vandalism as meaningless behaviour did not facilitate attempts to understand the phenomenon. Instead, they developed what came to be known as 'the subcultural theory' of delinquency which claims that certain types of behaviour such as vandalism are likely to be more prevalent in working-class neighbourhoods. "The major contribution of this approach", wrote Rutter and Giller (1983, p 247), "has been the recognition that some forms of (at least minor) delinquent behaviour constitute an accepted part of the social activities of adolescents". The fact that the vast majority of vandals and delinquents grow up, get married and settle down without becoming hardened criminals is advanced to show that their adolescent depradations are better characterised as temporary aberrations rather than as evidence of pathological disturbance or social maladjustment. Indeed, John Barron Mays claimed (1954) that in certain districts of Liverpool it was the boy who did not become delinquent who was more likely to be maladjusted.

In the late 1960s a group of more radical sociologists developed what they termed a more sceptical, 'interactionist' perspective to crime, deviance and social problems. The deviancy symposium, associated with such names as Stan Cohen, Laurie Taylor, Jock Young and Paul Walton, introduced into this country the notions of labelling theory, where the focus of attention is shifted from the original deviant act to the reactions of society and the processes by which deviants come to be labelled by others. It was a reaction against the psychologist's "...obsessive game of finding the holy grail which will tell us the secret of deviance...The only part left out of this picture is the deviant himself and the fact that he arrives at his position and becomes the sort of person he is through a series of processes observable elsewhere in life. It is these processes we are interested in, not just the initial pushes and pulls but the stages of involvement, disinvolvement, side-tracking, doubt, guilt and commitment" (Cohen, 1971, p 18).

The third approach to the study of vandalism is based on the notion that crime can be prevented architecturally. Much of the success of Oscar

Newman's (1972) book *Defensible Space* is, I think, to be explained by the power and impact of a snappy, new concept, 'defensible space', on a neglected topic - the connections between architectural design and crime. The major characteristics of defensible space, according to Newman, are that public housing can be designed to encourage residents to supervise, take responsibility for and defend their buildings from strangers; and that design can lessen the isolation and stigma of such housing if it is also located between areas which are relatively 'safe' from crime. Newman's thesis has attracted considerable attention over the years and much of it has been critical (eg Bottoms, 1974; Mawby, 1977; and Mayhew, 1979). He himself in later publications such as *Community of Interest* in 1980 admitted that other factors beside physical design affected crime rates in housing projects and he mentioned specifically the socio-economic characteristics of residents, the degree of shared values and life-styles among them and the policies of housing managers. More recently, Colin Ward (1990, p 6) has rightly praised Newman for having stimulated much valuable research and for having been "absolutely on the side of the tenants".

At the same time as the central notions of defensible space were being put to the empirical test, a group of environmental psychologists began to argue that the three hypotheses which we have introduced so far - the psychological, the sociological and the architectural - failed to explain a number of key facts concerning vandalism and so a fourth approach began to emerge, that of the socio-environmental system. Why, for instance, are certain schools and telephone kiosks repeatedly attacked by vandals, while other schools and call-boxes serving similar areas or located in the very same neighbourhood remain relatively unscathed? How do people decide which spaces are public or semi-public and so fair game to be vandalised? How does the appearance of vandalism so change the relationship between individuals and their environment that it so often leads to an increase in vandalism which progressively worsens the living conditions for everyone, including the vandals themselves? Claude Levy-Leboyer, who organised the first international conference on vandalism at the Université Rene Descartes in Paris in October, 1982, has advanced this new school of thought which she explains (1984, p 9) as an "...individual/environment system, with the environment being viewed as a sociophysical whole, and not one of individuals on the one hand and the environment on the other."

An example may help to clarify this rather cryptic statement. In a cleverly designed study, Moser (1984, p 174) tested the reactions of users to malfunctioning public telephones in Paris and in small towns and under two conditions - sometimes their money was returned and on other occasions it was withheld. In Paris "...people were found to be more aggressive than in small towns: they handled telephones roughly more often, and they stayed in booths longer when money was withheld than when money was returned...Lack of control over the environment appears to intensify aggressive behaviour in telephone booths, but only in urban environments".

The approach taken in this report is an unashamedly eclectic one, which will present a personal account of, and selection from, the published work of all four schools of thought: none of them appears to me to have a monopoly of good theoretical ideas or of effective preventative measures. Many researchers, moreover, do not fit neatly into one of the four rough categories outlined above and tend to use ideas and methods which are drawn from a number of approaches. I have also tried to learn from the Cyril Burt fiasco which was in part caused by academics like myself relying extensively on second hand sources rather than reading the original texts. Writing this report has also taken me into areas such as housing policy where I have no expertise.

This introductory chapter ends with a brief examination of what is considered by the Home Office Research Unit to be the main features of vandalism in this country and an account of what consensus can be found in the literature. The Research Unit has for some years been carrying out a programme of research "...initiated because of increasing public concern with the problem of vandalism" (Croft, 1978, p iii). According to one of their senior scientific officers, Ron Clarke, writing in 1978 (p 68):

> ...the nature of vandalism is that it consists essentially of an accumulation of innumerable rather petty incidents of graffiti, broken windows, defaced road signs, uprooted shrubs, and telephones put out of action. The main result of this damage is to impoverish the environment.

Three further points are stressed -

> ...a comparatively small proportion of vandalism appears to be committed against people's personal or private property...most vandalism is directed at local authority property (Clarke, 1978, p 68).

...most of the vandalism seems to be committed either by young children in the course of unsupervised play, or by older adolescents seeking prestige and excitement; relatively little seems to be committed by older youths or adults (Ibid, p 69).

...The motivation underlying vandalism by adolescent youths may also fuel other forms of delinquent behaviour, especially theft... (Ibid, p 69).

These excerpts will now be scrutinised in order to make two general points. First, what is to count as vandalism is ultimately a political question. The official view quoted above would have us believe that vandalism is <u>in essence</u> nothing more than the petty damage committed by young children and adolescents. The Home Office Research Unit, although it has produced some of the most quoted publications, all of which are based on its strictly limited definition of vandalism, has never studied, for example: "...the vast and devastating effects of the activities of local authorities and speculative developers in destroying traditional environments" (Ward, 1990, p 1). When discussing the problems of deciding what should count as vandalism, their tactic has been to employ a body swerve worthy of a rugby three-quarter; witness Ron Clarke's response to Ward's claim, which, he wrote (1978, p 2), "...raises important issues about the ambit of the criminal law which fall outside the scope of the research described in this volume".

Furthermore, there is no hint in the official version that the "...stereotypical profile of the vandal as a 'working-class inner-city male adolescent' has been invalidated by various studies. **Vandals come from urban and suburban as well as rural areas, from working-class and middle-class as well as upper-class families, and are of different ethnic origins** (van Vliet, 1984, p 14). **A recognition of the growing involvement of girls in vandalism** (Stone and Taylor, 1977; Pollard, 1988) **would also help to correct the stereotype**: girls were, for instance, simply excluded from Gladstone's self-report study, mentioned earlier, which was part of the Home Office's research programme into vandalism.

Is there, then, nothing in the literature which has attracted general agreement and approval? Is it all conflict and criticism? The first book devoted exclusively to the topic of *Juvenile Vandalism: A Study of Its Nature and Prevention* was written by John Martin, an Assistant Professor of Sociology at Fordham University, New York City, in 1961. In the thirty years which have passed since, only one law has been established which has been generally accepted - the architect Peter Shepheard's Law of

Diminishing Vandalism which claims that **"persistence in replanting and replacing destroyed plants until the children get tired of destruction or learn better" is rapidly repaid**. Colin Ward (1990, p 9) continues his discussion of Shepheard's Law as follows:

> ...*Allan Blenkarn, recreational services manager for British Waterways Board applied this theory: 'Vandals smash a place up at the weekend. Repair it first thing on Monday morning. They come again next weekend. Repair it again. The third weekend they probably won't come back again'. A much more recent application of this approach is in the vast shopping centre at Central Milton Keynes. It is vandal-free, just because of endless replacement and continual supervision.*

There is only one other thread which runs consistently through most of the relevant literature: **a strain of hypocritical moralising about the social depradations of the young**. Why hypocritical? After the publication of Ward's book on vandalism in 1973 both he and Stan Cohen received

> ...*endless requests to address meetings of councillors, community associations and chief constables. Comparing notes we found that they followed a pattern. The chairman would begin by stressing the dreadful social cost of environmental destruction, but later, over the coffee, would tell us about the terrible things he used to do as a young tearaway, but making no connections between then and now (Ward, 1990, p 3).*

Douglas Hurd, as Home Secretary, addressed a conference on vandalism in London in 1988 and argued that "...it is easy to see how today's young vandal can become tomorrow's football hooligan and next week's mugger" (1988, p 2). The anecdotal evidence of conference chairmen would suggest instead that the young vandals of yesteryear have become today's community leaders, chief constables and politicians.

None of the above should be interpreted as either passive acceptance or active encouragement of vandalism which, in some housing estates, schools and public places, has reached levels which the local residents (and most readers for that matter) would find intolerable. We all have a right to be brought up and to be educated in decent accommodation and to be free from the fear of being attacked or of our property being damaged; and yet these very basic rights are currently being denied to many of our fellow citizens. The GLC Police Committee (1984, p 11) collected evidence of vandalism on its housing estates and I shall quote briefly from two of the

When vandalism is coupled with racial harassment, then the majority of us have little, if any, understanding of what some families have to endure.

written submissions to the panel of enquiry:

> *The windows and doors in the foyer are continually being broken, the stairs are an absolute disgrace, the lifts are appalling, and as if this were not enough to contend with, our garages are continually being broken into and cars wrecked.*

Another tenant described living conditions in similar terms:

> *Following three weeks of having my telephone wires cut four times and my door bell cut, I have now had three bricks smashed through my front door and kitchen windows in the last two days. Graffiti has covered the front door frame and windows; its been written in stair wells and on verandah walls. The police have been called several times...*

We all know of such housing estates which we prefer to drive past and forget about, secure in the knowledge that none of our relatives and friends are forced to make a home and bring up children in such squalid and neglected places. But when vandalism is coupled with racial harassment, then the majority of us have little, if any, understanding of what some families have to endure. Witness the submission of an Indian family living in a London maisonette, again, to the GLC (1984, p 15):

> *We have had bottles thrown through one of our living room windows twice; eggs, mud and small pebbles thrown at our windows during the day and at night, also mud, dirt, rubbish and smoke bombs put in through our letterbox at any odd times. Also obscene language spray-painted in large block capitals on our front door asking us to go 'home'.*

Tony Harrison (1985, p 10) has imaginatively tried to understand what the crude slogans of skinheads reveal about them and their brutal environment in his poem *V*, where he also tried to come to terms with his own feelings at finding that his parents' grave in Leeds had been vandalised:

But why inscribe these graves with CUNT and SHIT?
Why choose neglected tombstones to disfigure?
This pitman's of last century daubed paki git,
this grocer Broadbent's aerosolled with NIGGER?

They're there to shock the living, not arouse
the dead from their deep peace to lend support
for the causes skinhead spraycans could espouse.
The dead would want their desecrators caught!

Jobless though they are how can these kids,
even though their team's lost one more game,
believe that the 'Pakis', 'Niggers', even 'Yids'
sprayed on the tombstones here should bear the blame?

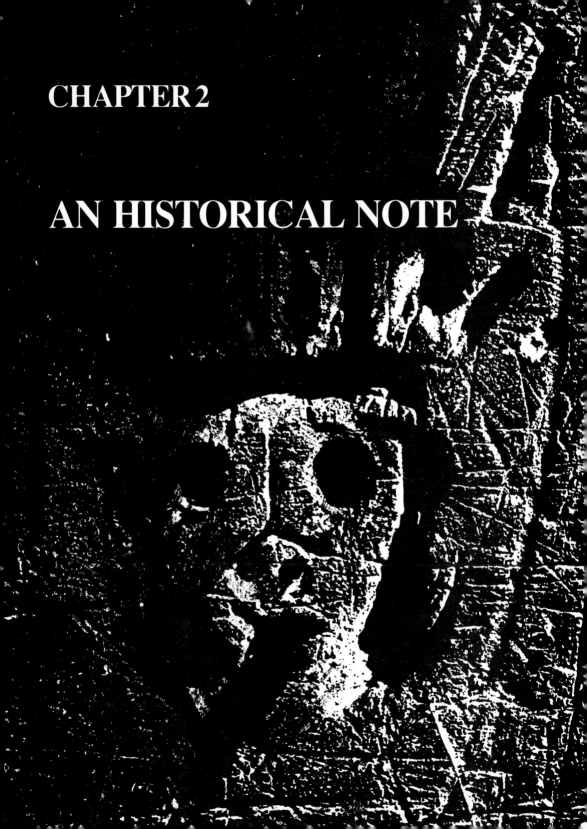

CHAPTER 2

AN HISTORICAL NOTE

The first modern use of the term 'vandalism' is explained by Simon Schama (1989) in his book *Citizens: A Chronicle of the French Revolution*. The term was coined by Henri Grégoire, the Bishop of Blois, to describe the acts of what Schama calls (p 829) "indiscriminate" destruction characteristic of the extreme phase of the Terror. But the assaults of the sans-culottes were anything but indiscriminate; for example, the wholesale destruction of the royal tombs in the Saint Denis chapel. Stories of the revolutionaries playing skittles with the bones of the Bourbon kings are judged by Schama to have been apocryphal, but the ransacking of Saint Denis had been authorised by a decree of the Convention of 1793. So, right from the first use of the word, the category of planned and deliberate ideological vandalism, as Stan Cohen calls it, was recognised.

Grégoire also saw education as the main approach to prevention and control; he "pressed on the Committee of Public Instruction an activist program which would turn back the vandal hordes from the gates of the new Rome..." (Schama, p 829). Robespierre's aim of enrolling an entire nation in the school of virtue by wielding a very big stick was no more successful in eighteenth century France than it has proved in late twentieth century Britain. "Plus ça change, c'est plus la même chose."

Allen develops this point adding that when the Abbé Grégoire was discussing his invention of the word "vandalisme" in his memoirs, he wrote: "Je créai le mot pour tuer la chose". Allen (1984, p 77) then comments:

> At the present time - almost 200 years later - we find that the good Abbé's word is still being widely and actively used not only by researchers, but by the mass media and the public in general. The continued wide currrency of this term attests to the fact that, unfortunately, 'le mot' did not successfully 'tuer la chose'.

The term 'vandalism' takes its origins, however, from the Vandals, who developed mailed cavalry and who were armed with lance and bow. They crossed the Rhine in AD 406 and three years later invaded Spain. They then built a fleet, overran the Balearic Islands, and restored the power of Carthage. Having attacked Sicily and Sardinia, they sacked the city of Rome in 455 by sailing up the Tiber. Although their sacking of Rome is described by the Oxford Classical Dictionary as "comparatively mild" (a verdict which I suspect the Romans of the time would have had something to say about), around AD 1700 their name became synonymous with a lack of culture, with rude, barbarous behaviour and with the ruthless destruction or spoiling of anything beautiful or venerable.

Barbarians have, however, had a bad press in the West for over two thousand years. Elaine Morgan in her book on the rise and decline of urban civilisation makes use of Biblical sources to show that the destruction of the barbarous Vandals was as nothing compared to "the venom of the civilized". She is worth quoting at length (1978, pp 84-85):

> It is rather ironical that the word 'vandalism' derives from the name of a barbarian, envisaged in most people's minds as an uncouth nomad storming in and defacing buildings and monuments whose beauty he was too boorish to appreciate. Very likely, but the efforts of the vandals and their kind have always been pathetically amateurish compared to the venom of the civilised who perceive the beauty and the splendour all too well and were maddened by it, as Sennacherib was by Babylon. When the looting was over he boasted 'the city and its houses from its foundations to its top I destroyed, I devastated, I burned with fire. The wall and the outer wall, temples and gods, temple towers of bricks and earth, as many as they were I razed and dumped into the Arakhtu Canal. Through the midst of that city I dug canals, I flooded its site with water and the very foundations thereof I destroyed...'

> Our own destructiveness - Coventry, Dresden, Hiroshima, Stalingrad - is more efficient still, and more elaborately rationalised these days. But it was only in the last century that Marshal Blucher, upon first clapping eyes on the City of London, uttered the spontaneous exclamation which could have come from any visiting soldier in any city right back through history: 'What a place to plunder!'

Roman soldiers scratched graffiti into tiles along Hadrian's Wall in Northumberland and, even earlier, their counterparts disfigured the tombs of the Egyptian pharaohs. **If this historical digression has made the point that vandalism was not invented by groups of male working-class adolescents in the London Underground in the 1960s, then it will have served its purpose.**

CHAPTER 3

DEFINE OR BE DEFINED!

"In the animal kingdom, the rule is eat or be eaten; in the human kingdom, define or be defined" (Thomas Szasz, quoted by Cohen, 1984a, p 55).

What is to count as vandalism? The answer, as we shall see, is by no means obvious because **there is no universally accepted definition**. Van Vliet (1984, p 31) presents the difficulty in a memorable way: "This issue of what gets labelled as vandalism, and what does not, is nicely captured in the observation: 'If a car hits a child, that is an accident, but if a child damages a car, that is vandalism'." Van Vliet's remark is superficially attractive but is also far too glib and asymmetrical. If a car happens to hit a child, that is <u>not</u> vandalism but an accident; even if the child had been deliberately run over, who would apply the term 'vandalism' to such an act? If, on the other hand, a child deliberately damages a car, that <u>is</u> vandalism. We need to determine, if possible, the motives and state of the driver (a momentary lapse of attention? or drunken driving?), and of the child (accidentally scraping paint off the side panel of a car with the handlebars of a bike? or deliberately with a pound coin?). The power to define the behaviour as either accidental or malicious damage becomes crucial.

Marsh et al (1978) use vandalism as their main example when they are explaining why supporters of labelling theory insist that deviance is created and sustained by the <u>reaction</u> of the community to an act of deviance. What, at first thought, appears to be a straightforward, obvious and neutral act - defining the behaviour of a group of hooligans as malicious damage - involves us in a series of decisions which reflect our moral, social and political (with a small 'p') values and which may have serious consequences for those we choose to define as vandals. As Marsh et al (1978, p 10) express it:

> *Vandalism, for example, might be thought of as a collection of clearly identifiable acts requiring sanction for the simple reason that they offend against the property, both individual and collective, of members in society. But contrast the reaction to football fans who run through a town creating damage as they go with the reaction to university students during rag week creating similar damage. The former damage will be viewed as the result of 'destructive hooliganism' and dealt with accordingly, whilst the latter will be seen as arising from an excess of good-natured high spirits and over-enthusiasm. Although the damaging acts are very similar, football fans are 'deviants' whilst students, for reasons not made explicit, are somehow excused.*

Some readers may feel that it is stretching a point to lump together the 'harmless' excesses of students who may hold up traffic while collecting for charity on rag days and the indiscriminate damage and terror caused by football hooligans rampaging through a city centre. Let me intensify the comparison. I have seen drunken university students systematically kick pint beer glasses through the windows of fellow students with virtual impunity; college officers took no further action beyond insisting on payment (by parents' cheque) for the damage done. Later in this chapter Cohen's arguments, which have convinced me at least, will be deployed to explain why the label of vandal is used under certain circumstances and of certain members of society and not of others.

Vandalism has been studied from at least four perspectives (see Chapter 1 for explanation), each employing a variety of methods in a large number of countries over many years. One of the reasons why this vast input of funds, effort and thought has not led to a systematic and cumulative body of knowledge is the wide range of practical problems researchers have experienced in studying **such a slippery concept as vandalism**. I list below some of the principal problems:

1. DIFFERENT DEFINITIONS

Some researchers define vandalism as anything which "...ranges from arson to graffiti" (Mayhew et al, 1989), but exclude incidents such as letting down car tyres because they are considered to be nuisance only. Others such as Clarke (1978, p 2) wish to restrict the term to deal with "deliberate or malicious damage (excluding serious cases of arson)". In a survey of hooliganism and breakdowns in public order, 22% of those members of the public who were interviewed defined their fears of being robbed or attacked in the street as vandalism (see Clarke, 1978, p 2). And were the workers who substituted the exhortation "Fuck Off" for "Blackpool" in half a mile of sticky rock indulging in vandalism or industrial sabotage (see Taylor and Walton, 1971)? How are leaking roofs which may have been damaged as a result of an attempted break-in to be categorised? Are pupils who scratch their names on school property to be considered vandals or is this very common activity (85% of schoolboys admit to it, according to Gladstone, 1978) to be written off as routine wear and tear? If the former, how are we to explain the obvious pride of public schools such as Harrow which treat the initials carved by Robert Clive and Winston Churchill as "part of a routine which enhanced the sense of historical continuity" (Ward, 1973, p 294)? **The vandalism of the last century becomes today's tourist attraction**.

2. OPERATIONAL DEFINITIONS AND DIFFICULTIES

Such conceptual confusion and temporal relativity are shunned by those researchers who opt for a workable definition which will impose some consistency and validity on their findings. Sheena Wilson (1980, p 47), for example, in her study of vandalism and defensible space on London housing estates took vandalism to mean damage to property caused by:

a) accident eg a football through a window

b) direct attack eg from an air gun, or

c) misuse-cum-play eg swinging on doors until they come off their hinges.

Most researchers have tended to omit accidental damage from their definition, preferring to include it in the category of wear and tear which Wilson certainly excluded. Her inclusion of accidents is all the more puzzling since she goes on to claim "...no attempt was made (nor indeed would it have been possible) to differentiate the effects of intentional damage from those of less deliberate rowdyism". The practical problem is one which Wilson is clearly aware of: **how are we to decide after the event whether the damage was committed maliciously or not?** As Zwier and Vaughan (1984, p 266) comment: "One can never be sure that a broken window is due to malicious intent, unless the vandal is caught in flagrante delictu". Their study of school vandalism reports that Panko collected 2,516 different definitions from teachers and arrived at the following definition of school vandalism: "...unauthorized intentional damage and theft of school and district property, excluding theft for material gain of the actor and associated damages, if any". The differences between Panko's and Wilson's definitions are obvious, and there is nothing to stop another researcher, fresh to the field, developing yet another definition and collecting data on another sub-grouping of the general problem.

Furthermore, Mawby (1977, p 34) found, while studying vandalised telephone kiosks in Sheffield, that the definition of vandalism was left to the repairer so that damage caused by accidental breakages or wear and tear may often have been wrongly labelled as vandalism. The impact on the validity of his data is likely to have been considerable and to have come from two sources. First, when repairers have been particularly sensitised to an outbreak of vandalism either through media campaigns or managerial pressure, they may "label more damage as due to vandalism, and thereby create a spurious rise in the figures". Second, "repairers come to define certain kiosks as 'high risk' and are therefore more likely to label incidents in them as caused by vandalism" (Ibid).

3. INFLATION AND DEFLATION OF THE FIGURES

The literature contains numerous incidents where the figures for vandalism may have been either deliberately inflated or under-reported for reasons which, however understandable, muddy the statistical waters still further. Gladstone (1980, p 143) gives instances of both tendencies:

> ...a significant amount of the damage labelled 'vandalism' occurred accidentally, a typical example being a football through a window. [Notice that his colleague in the Home Office Resesarch Unit, Sheena Wilson, includes such accidents in her definition of vandalism, as quoted above.] In some cases accidental damage was called 'vandalism' because the headmaster or caretaker believed (erroneously, it is said) that vandalism was repaired more quickly than wear and tear.

Here the separate categories are being deliberately manipulated because the fabric and appearance of the buildings are obviously more important to practitioners than any spurious rise in the statistics.

Gladstone also reports that other heads preferred not to make public that their school was being damaged by vandals, no doubt to avoid adverse publicity and to protect the reputation of their schools. **How much reliance can we then place on statistics when they are at the mercy of such subjective judgments and mixed motives?** Sturman (1978, p 14) also encountered the problem of overlap or multiple counting: when residents were interviewed about damage to their property "...it was not always possible to tell whether different people were reporting the same incident or not".

To sum up at this point, researchers have found that **those who provide data for statistics on vandalism are operating with widely different definitions, they tend to make subjective judgments about what to include and exclude with obvious implications for the validity of research findings,** and the final figures may also have been subject to deliberate inflation, deflation or multiple reporting of a simple incident.

4. COMPARATIVE DIFFERENCES

As if we did not have enough to contend with already, comparative studies show that some countries include in their legal definition of vandalism behaviour which is categorised as theft or burglary elsewhere. Moser et al (1984, p 247) illustrate this point exactly: "In France, for instance, juvenile courts place the breaking up of school furniture, the smashing of window panes in public buildings and breaking and entering into one and the same category". Markus (1984, p 312) actually claims that the level of vandalism to public payphones in the UK was four times the level of that in France in 1982. That is an intriguing finding worthy of further investigation but trust in these figures is suspended when he claims further that, in the same year, there were more than thirty-one times as many thefts of cash from payphones in France than in the UK. The most obvious conclusion is that like is not being compared with like and I suspect problems of definition are at the root of the disparity. John Martin (1961, p 4) even quotes definitions of vandalism by American criminologists who have restricted the term to the deliberate destruction of property "by a juvenile or group of juveniles", as though the vandalism of adults in, say, environmental pollution could be safely disregarded. **How can meaningful comparative studies be carried out when such definitional differences exist?**

It is therefore no wonder that Claude Levy-Leboyer concluded (1984, p 2) that **the concept of vandalism "...is in fact a ragbag in which highly diverse types of behaviour are to be found under one and the same name"**. If we accept the four types of difficulty encountered by researchers which have been explained above, "...we end up with the uncomfortable recognition that vandalism is neither a precise behavioural description, nor a recognisable legal category, but a label attached to certain types of behaviour under certain conditions" (Cohen, 1973, p 23). As so often, Stan Cohen has come to the rescue not only by stating what those conditions are but also by outlining six types of vandalism. This chapter will end with a brief exposition of his classificatory system.

Cohen (1973, p 23) argues that acts of vandalism are best viewed as being on a continuum from, at the one end, behaviour which is invariably labelled and processed as criminal to, at the other, types of illegal property destruction which are socially tolerated. There are six conditions, according to Cohen, which explain why "institutionalized rule-breaking" becomes acceptable and these he calls: ritualism, protection, play, writing-off, walling-in and licensing, each of which will be briefly explained.

a. Ritualism: special occasions like Guy Fawkes night, Hogmanay, Hallowe'en and stag parties when property destruction is condoned or even encouraged.

b. Protection: groups (of students, particularly) who are given a collective licence by the community to let off steam and whose vandalism is later labelled 'ill-judged'. Such protection is awarded on a social class basis and involves political criteria, as the example from Marsh et al (1978), about the differential treatment of football fans and university students at the beginning of this chapter, makes explicit.

c. Play: the breaking of windows or milk bottles or building materials on a construction site by young children as part of a game.

d. Writing-off: minor property defacement such as writing on the walls of toilets in pubs which is ignored or written off because it is so pervasive and predictable.

e. Walling-in: property destruction which is contained and sanctioned within the walls of an institution like a prison, university college or mental hospital (that is, if you can tell the difference between these 'total' institutions). The frequent smashing up of furniture within prisons would constitute a good example, especially when such vandalism is dealt with internally.

f. Licensing: "An example of licensed vandalism is the type of damage done to hotels by resident sporting teams, especially during sports festivals" (Cohen, 1973, p 33), where the culprits are allowed to pay for the repairs by organising a whip-round rather than being formally charged with criminal damage.

5. TYPOLOGIES OF VANDALISM

The first book on the topic by John Martin (1961) suggested a general typology of vandalism which divided it, like Gaul, into three parts: predatory, vindictive and wanton vandalism. Since then there have been a number of attempts to produce a definitive classification and these have been collected by van Vliet (1984, pp 18-19). Unfortunately his list degenerates into a catalogue of particular instances of vandalism such as the mutilation and theft of library periodicals. For my money, the six types of vandalism outlined by Cohen (1973a) has not been bettered, although researchers like Baker and Waddon (1989) claim to have adapted and extended his original list; but to add the category of "graffiti", to omit that of "tactical vandalism", and to change the name of "vindictive vandalism" to "problem expression" is simply to tinker at the edges to no great purpose and so I wish to retain Cohen's formulation which is as follows:

a. **Ideological Vandalism: property is destroyed to gain publicity for a particular cause and is justified by long-standing grievances or political beliefs.** Perhaps one of the most famous historical cases of ideological vandalism is the Reichstag Fire of 1933 which was started by the young Dutchman Marinus van der Lubbe who said to the German police "At the outset I must insist that my action was inspired by political motives..." (Graham, 1970, p 8). Far from being an arsonist or a tool of the Nazis, his own account makes clear that he was a Communist who thought that the "intimidated masses" would shake off their lethargy if they saw one of the "strongholds of capitalism" going up in flames. Whether the perpetrators are labelled heroes or hooligans, visionaries or vandals depends on the same political processes which determine whether a member of the Irish Republican Army who plants a bomb in a London railway station is called a 'terrorist' or a 'freedom fighter'. Similarly, Saddam Hussein is seen either as 'the butcher of Baghdad' or 'the leader of pan-Arab nationalism' depending on which view you take of the origins of the Gulf War.

b. **Acquisitive Vandalism: to acquire money or property** by, for instance, stripping lead from church roofs, looting telephone coin boxes, or collecting traffic cones or police signs.

c. **Tactical Vandalism: a means of achieving some other end**, like breaking the window of a major store in order to secure in prison a warm bed and food for the winter, or bringing a production line to a stop to provide some respite from the monotony of the job.

d. **Vindictive Vandalism: to get revenge**, to get one's own back, or to settle a grudge eg smashing school furniture to express anger over privileges being withdrawn or popular pupils being excluded.

e. **Play Vandalism: fun or 'high spirits'** which is not interpreted as breaking any rules and which is motivated by curiosity or competition to see who, for example, can break the most windows in a deserted building.

f. **Malicious Vandalism: the category which many people fail to understand because it appears to be vicious, apparently meaningless** and carried out in the main by groups of working-class youths on publicly-owned property. For Cohen, malicious vandalism is the behaviour of young people who are "...<u>breaking</u> out, <u>breaking</u> away and <u>breaking</u> clear" (1973a, p 49, emphasis as in original). For such young people vandalism is the ideal form of rule breaking because it allows them, caught as they are at "the edge of impotent rage", to express their deeply felt feelings of frustration, failure, boredom or despair in acts of provocative violence which cost them little, as so few of them are ever convicted.

CONCLUSION

At this point a reader may - with some justification - ask why so much space has been devoted to what could be dismissed as an academic, semantic quibble over the definition of the one word 'vandalism'. I hope sufficient has been said already to make clear that defining certain members of society as vandals is not a neutral but a political act with serious consequences for those so defined, for those who have the power to define others, and for social policy more generally. In debates about whether the definition of vandalism should be extended to include, say, the damage caused by local authorities and speculative developers we are engaged in a struggle over whose version of social reality will prevail. And **the act of definition has been called 'political' because it is impossible to study vandalism for any length of time without realising that what often lies behind the immediate discussion is either control over housing or the educational and occupational opportunities of large sections of the population. In short, the debate over vandalism needs to be connected to wider issues such as power, conflict and sectional interests within society.** Quoting the legal definition of vandalism will not help us to explain why certain people can break the law with impunity and Cohen's six conditions under which rule breaking is tolerated are not available to all and sundry but only to certain protected groups in society. Sudden outbreaks of vandalism may be more explicable either in terms of the impact of factory closures on certain working-class communities where unemployment is already high or the annual charity rag day of university students which gets out of hand.

The disarray among researchers, each of whom develops his or her favourite definition or series of definitions over the years, means that studies are neither strictly comparable nor cumulative. It would be a considerable advance if a self-denying ordinance were to be entered into by the whole research community, **whereby one definition and typology were to be chosen as the basis for future work** and Cohen's typology is the most obvious candidate. Such a move would not, however, be a panacea because Cohen's categories tend to overlap and are not strictly discrete; tactical vandalism, for instance, could on occasions also be classified as ideological and the boundary between vindictive and malicious vandalism is at times rather arbitrary. Yet, if any sophisticated statistical techniques (from correlation co-efficients onwards) are to be employed to tease out relationships between vandalism and, say, truancy, then discrete classifications are necessary. The transitory and ambiguous nature of much vandalism, the myriad definitions of the term used in research studies, and the arbitrary character of so many decisions about what is to count as vandalism, would all suggest that the role of statistical analysis will always be rather limited. This takes us to our next theme - what can we learn about vandalism from official statistics?

CHAPTER 4

OFFICIAL STATISTICS ON PREVALENCE AND COST

What can be learned from studying official statistics on vandalism? *Criminal Statistics, England and Wales 1989*, which was published in November 1990, states that 630,000 offences of criminal damage were reported to the police in 1989, amounting to 16.2% of the total of 3.7 million notifiable offences which were recorded in that year, a 6% increase on the previous year. Offences of criminal damage have almost doubled since 1979 (from 320,500

Figure 4.1

<u>Notifiable offences recorded by the police per 100, 000 population in England and Wales.</u>

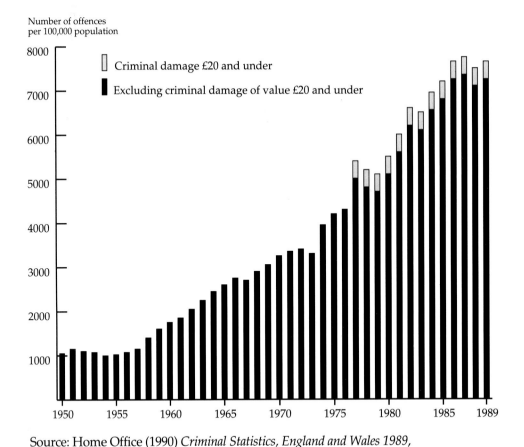

Number of offences
per 100,000 population

Source: Home Office (1990) *Criminal Statistics, England and Wales 1989*, London: HMSO, Cm 1322, p 22

to 630,000) and, if 1980 is preferred as the base year for calculations because a revised set of counting rules was introduced then, the increase in the years up to 1989 was 75%.

Figure 4.1 illustrates rather dramatically the huge rise in the total number of offences recorded by the police from around 500,000 in the early 1950s to 3.7 million in 1989; **about 3 million of that increase were offences against property**. To express the same finding in different words, over the last forty years there has been a seven fold increase in the number of offences recorded by the police - the rate per 100,000 population has moved steadily upwards from around 1,100 in 1950 to about 7,400 in 1989. Such long-term comparisons are, however, fraught with difficulty and the change which was introduced in 1977, whereby offences of criminal damage of value £20 or less are recorded separately, is a case in point. This change has introduced further complications because each year more minor offences cross the £20 limit through the effects of inflation. The argument is taken further in *Criminal Statistics* (Home Office, 1990, p 21): "This not only inflates the rate of increase of the recorded numbers but also tends to cause the clear-up rate to

The incidence of vandalism varies markedly from one part of the country to another...

Table 4.1

Criminal damage per 100,000 population by area

Police Force Area	All Criminal Damage	Percentage Change
Cleveland	1,724	+6
Cumbria	918	+2
Durham	1,622	+5
Merseyside	1,352	+5
Metropolitan Police District	1,773	+5
Northumbria	2,257	+37
North Yorkshire	644	+3
Surrey	646	-
England and Wales (average)	1,250	+6

Extracted from Tables 2.6 and 2.7 from Home Office (1990), *Criminal Statistics, England and Wales 1989,* London: HMSO, Cm 1322, pp 38-9

fall because minor offences are in general less likely to be cleared up than more serious ones".

Interestingly, the levels of offences of criminal damage vary markedly from one part of the country to another, or, to be more precise, from one police force area to another. I have extracted the figures for all criminal damage per 100,000 population for a number of northern and London police forces and added the percentage change since 1988 and presented the results in Table 4.1. It comes as no surprise that the Metropolitan Police District (which, in this case, includes the City of London) scores more highly than the average for England and Wales, but the figures for Cleveland, Durham and especially Northumbria (the highest in the whole country, with a percentage change more than double any other police force) take some explaining. The rates for Surrey and North Yorkshire, respectively the lowest and second lowest in England and Wales, clearly suggest some social class differences. Offences of criminal damage, as a percentage of all recorded crime, have risen from 12.6% in 1979 to 16.2% in 1989, and over the same period **the detection and clear-up rate has fallen from 30% to 23% to make it the lowest detection rate of any category of crime**.

Figure 4.2 shows that in 1989 young people under the age of 21 accounted for more than 50% of all those found guilty of or cautioned for offences of

Figure 4.2

Persons found guilty of, or cautioned for, indictable offences by offence group and age

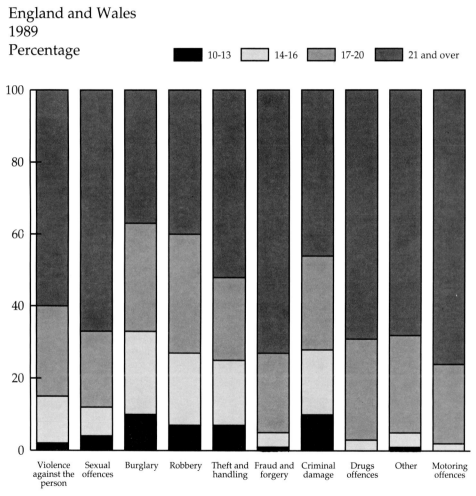

England and Wales
1989
Percentage

Source: Home Office (1990) *Criminal Statistics, England and Wales 1989,*
London: Cm 1322 p 92

39

criminal damage and, perhaps more worryingly, of burglary, robbery, theft and handling stolen goods. It is also true, of course, that around 44% of all those found guilty of, or cautioned for, offences of criminal damage were over 21 years-old and this point will be picked up in the final chapter. Those brought to court and found guilty of criminal damage were predominantly male, 8,600 in 1979 (a figure which rose to only 8,700 in 1989), compared with 600 females in 1979 (and only 700 in 1989).

The statistics quoted above have all the appearance of being objective, correct and convincing; but do they, for instance accurately reflect the amount of crime which is actually being committed? The annual report from the Home Office (1990, p 19) claims that the statistics recorded by the police "...provide only a partial picture of crime committed", partly because many offences are not reported to the police and partly because the police decide not to record others. Although there are detailed counting rules which are issued centrally and followed by all police forces, there still remains a large area for local discretion over which incidents are to be considered genuine, serious and worthy of recording. Even then, as we have seen already, how is a broken window to be classified? As the result of an accident, criminal damage or an attempted burglary? The very steep rise (of 37%) in the figures for all criminal damage in Northumbria, given in Table 4.1, may be explained by differences in the practice of local authorities in that area in their reporting of vandalism to public property; alternatively, a media campaign may have heightened the public's awareness of and sensitivity to this particular type of offence and so increased their willingness to report cases to the police.

To sum up, **official statistics of recorded crime contain well-known shortcomings, which are acknowledged by police and criminologists alike**: local discretion and even the number of police officers available will lead to variations in the counting and classifying of offences. The so-called 'dark figure' of crime is likely to be much larger than official statistics which are better viewed as a measure of police activity. Many victims do not report incidents because they consider them to be relatively trivial, or because they have not witnessed the offence at first hand, or because they do not trust the police, or because they believe there is little the police can do, particularly about such offences as vandalism. Moreover, some people are disinclined to become involved in court proceedings and elderly people can sometimes be afraid of victimisation.

Is there, however, any way of estimating more accurately the size and shape of the complete iceberg, whose visible section represents those crimes recorded by the police? British Crime Surveys (BCS) have been conducted in England and Wales in 1982, 1984 and 1988. The latest survey (Mayhew et al, 1989, p 1) "...questions a large, random sample of the population aged 16 and over about offences they have experienced over the last year, whether or not these have been reported to the police". Figure 4.3 depicts the levels of recorded and unrecorded crime for 1987 by combining information from the BCS with police statistics. Clearly, **of all offence types, vandalism has by far the lowest percentage (10%) recorded in criminal statistics.** Three main reasons were given by respondents for not notifying the police: there had been little loss or damage (57%), the police could do nothing (26%) and the police would not be interested (12%). A comparison showed that in 1987 the police recorded 305,000 offences of criminal damage and BCS 2,931,000; the police gave the percentage change in such offences since 1981 as 52% and BCS as 9%, a statistically significant difference. The BCS report comments on these findings as follows: "Across the same years there has been a rise in the propensity to report vandalism incidents, and there is evidence that the level at which reported crimes are recorded has also increased. It may also be that the sharper rise in vandalism recorded by the police reflects an increasing tendency against classifying incidents as attempted burglary where the evidence is doubtful" (Mayhew et al, 1989, p 17).

I propose examining in more detail one attempt to measure vandalism in a city suburb to bring home the point that **official statistics on vandalism which at first sight appear objective, accurate and convincing can be quickly shown to be patchy, imprecise and misleading.** Sturman (1978) estimated the extent of vandalism on a large council housing estate in the suburbs of Manchester by comparing police records with those of the Post Office, and of the two local authority departments of Parks and Direct Works. In addition, interviews were held with tenants on the estate to obtain information about their experiences as victims; head teachers, shop managers and shop assistants were also surveyed to provide as comprehensive a picture of vandalism on the estate as possible.

Sturman (1978, p 16) reports his findings in this way:

> The surveys and Post Office records between them revealed some 14 to 15 times as much damage as police records. Compared to offences of criminal damage involving more than £20 which were recorded in the Criminal Statistics at the

Figure 4.3

Levels of recorded and unrecorded crime, 1987- British Crime Survey estimates

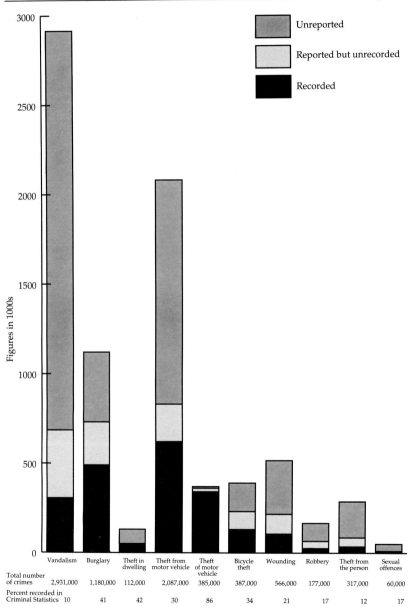

	Vandalism	Burglary	Theft in dwelling	Theft from motor vehicle	Theft of motor vehicle	Bicycle theft	Wounding	Robbery	Theft from the person	Sexual offences
Total number of crimes	2,931,000	1,180,000	112,000	2,087,000	385,000	387,000	566,000	177,000	317,000	60,000
Percent recorded in Criminal Statistics	10	41	42	30	86	34	21	17	12	17

Source: Mayhew, P et al (1989) *The 1988 British Crime Survey*, Home Office Research Study 111, London: HMSO, p 10

time of the study, the surveys and Post Office records between them revealed nearly 35 times as many incidents. Obviously police records give a very unreliable picture of the extent of vandalism except, perhaps, for the most costly incidents.

The finding that only 7% of incidents of vandalism were reported to the police and that 58% of these were of a minor nature concerning damage valued by the police at £20 or less should give pause for thought. While I was immersing myself in the literature on vandalism and, unfortunately, before I came across Sturman's work, I wrote to the chief constables of Northumbria, Durham, Cleveland, North Yorkshire and the Metropolitan Police Authority in London, asking for a breakdown of the figures for criminal damage for the years 1979 to 1989 as between adults and juveniles, males and females, etc... The major finding is that trying to extract information in this way was, with two splendid exceptions, like pulling teeth. I either received no reply (after repeated reminders), or was sent global figures for the years 1985 to 1989 which made comparisons impossible. One police force area reported that, although the 1989 figures for criminal damage had increased by 40% since 1985, the figures for one sub-division had risen by over 80% over that period - the rise was explained by a sudden influx of new residents onto housing estates in the sub-division. The quality and quantity of the data I received did not stand comparison with the official statistics which were discussed at the start of this chapter and so are not discussed further.

The main thrust of this chapter has, however, already been made: **official crime statistics are the final outcome of a long series of social processes and, at each stage along the way, decisions are made which can seriously inflate or deflate the figures.** Besides, criminal damage is a category of offence which is particularly susceptible to under-reporting and, consequently, the reservations which are rightly held about criminal statistics in general must be doubled in the case of vandalism.

More specifically, Sturman (1978, pp 16-18) reviewed the three main methods of collecting data on vandalism (by personal observation, by examining what records exist and by conducting surveys of victims), and concluded as follows: "...all techniques for measuring vandalism have limitations either in accuracy or comprehensiveness...police records provide neither an unbiased estimate of various types of vandalism nor a satisfactory estimate of the total amount".

THE COST OF VANDALISM

Commentators have not hesitated to estimate the financial burden of vandalism. In addition to the twenty sources listed by van Vliet (1984, p 15), which includes the claim made anonymously in 1979 to the United States Commission on Crime and Delinquency that vandalism was costing the US one billion dollars a year, I have collected a further twenty-one detailed estimates. Most of these claims share a number of characteristics: they are either vague ("...certainly in my own county of Merseyside last year, vandalism cost somewhere in the region of £11 million", Oxford, 1988, p 20); or they are exaggerated ("A figure of £870,000 was reached which was quickly rounded up by the press to 'This £1,000,000 Problem'", Pullen, 1973, p 259); or no indication is given of how the total has been arrived at ("Throughout England and Wales it is estimated that the bill for vandalism, arson and burglary [of schools] is running at more than £100 million a year", Dean and Read, 1990, p 1); or they prove difficult to reconcile (at the same conference on vandalism in 1988, a general manager from British Telecom claimed that "...on average, every payphone in the county will be attacked four times a year" (Green, 1988, p 7), while a researcher argued that "...a recent survey indicated that nationally 0.6% of the payphones were not working due to vandalism" (Giller, 1988, p 11).

To set against the majority of reports which emphasise that the costs of vandalism are both staggering and rising, there is a small body of more careful studies which have shown that the costs, when detailed, are at times moderate or at least not escalating. Mawby (1977, p 35), for example, found that the cost of vandalism to telephone kiosks in Sheffield amounted to 2.7% of kiosk income; nationally, the cost in 1976/77 represented 1.8% of kiosk income (Mayhew et al, 1980, p 74). If, as Gladstone (1980, p 157) demonstrated, the raw figures for school vandalism in Manchester between 1969 and 1977 are taken at face value, then the cost appears to have more than quadrupled (see Figure 4.4): "But, of course, over the period prices have risen considerably and where costs are adjusted for inflation, it becomes apparent that the real cost has risen little if at all" (see Figure 4.5).

Nothing has been said so far to suggest that the problem of vandalism has been so exaggerated that it can be safely ignored. Only a few figures are needed to counteract any such impression. In 1987 it cost British Telecom £18 million to replace damaged equipment and the labour to install it (Green, 1988, p 7); in the same year damage to property reported to the British

Figure 4.4

The rising price of vandalism to schools

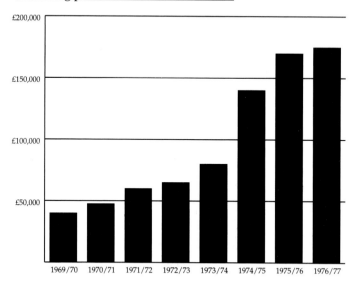

Figure 4.5

Total cost of school vandalism adjusted for inflation (all at 1976/77 prices)

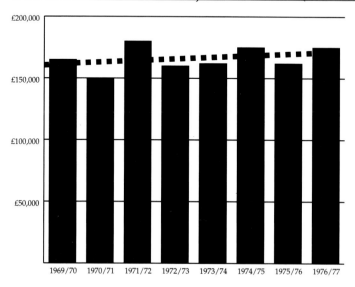

Source: Gladstone, FJ (1980) 'Co-ordinating Crime Prevention Efforts'

Transport Police amounted to £3,723,000 (McGregor, 1988, p 15); and "...it currently costs London Underground roughly £ 3-4 million per year to clean up trains, stations and structures like walls and bridges" (Ekblom, 1978, p 17). Damage to glazing alone in schools in England and Wales has recently been estimated by the Architects and Building branch of the DES (1990, p 3) to cost some £16 million to £18 million per annum. When the cost of arson in school buildings is calculated and the total restricted to large fires which cause more than £50,000 worth of damage, the figure was £11.1 million in 1985, over £30 million in 1986, and expected to be £50 million in 1989 (NERSSG, 1990, p 9). These are considerable sums by anyone's account and must be galling to those trying to maintain the physical fabric of our education system which is in urgent need of repair and capital investment quite apart from the damage created by deliberate fires. It needs to be said that **the money spent on repairing criminal damage or arson is money which is being diverted from other more worthy causes and is therefore in that sense being wasted**.

In addition to the direct monetary costs, the social costs must also be considered. Herbert (1990, p 65) writes of the psychological distress suffered by some teachers whose school had been burned down and gives examples of racial graffiti which sparked race riots and forced other schools to close. Vandalised playground equipment has also been implicated (by Burall, 1980) in the large number of accidents to children, requiring hospital treatment. NACRO (1988, p 14), in a study of young people growing up on housing estates, point to other indirect costs of vandalism and other forms of crime: "The financial costs to the courts, the police, prison and probation services and social service departments are considerable".

The final word is given to Stan Cohen (1973b, p 215) who argues that, beyond the direct monetary value of the damaged property, there is the symbolic value which

> *...is represented by the threat to the ethics surrounding the possession of property. An assault on property is an assault on those ethics, which in our society involve a complex set of rights, statuses and obligations. Certain forms of vandalism in addition threaten values surrounding the orderly resolution of racial, political and religious differences.*

CHAPTER 5

OF MOTIVES AND MEANINGS

There have been almost as many explanations offered for vandalism as there have been commentators. Armchair theorists have produced an extensive list of 'causes' or underlying motives which includes a sense of injustice (Baron and Fisher, 1984); inadequate custodial services, parental irresponsibility, and personality aberrations in the child (all cited by Goldman, 1961); ethnic prejudice against Puerto Rican youth in New York (Wade, 1967); and racial harassment in London as exemplified in racist slogans, abuse and violence (GLC, 1984). Some accounts describe a pretty lethal cocktail of psychological, sociological and environmental factors: boredom, frustration, lack of facilities, high expectations, rebellious tendencies, the failure of the home to transmit positive social values, the inadequacies of the educational and economic systems, the physical setting and the prevailing opportunity structure are all implicated in Washington Development Corporation's (1972) study of vandalism in the new town of that name in Sunderland.

Douglas Hurd, who was Home Secretary in 1988, addressed a conference on vandalism and began his discussion of causation by stating: "We are not dealing here with some protest movement, whether against the Government, police or society as a whole" (1988, p 2). Rather, in his view, the causes were boredom, "stupid drinking" and young people's "appetite for excitement".

The two previous paragraphs have listed seventeen possible explanations and it would not be difficult to take the total to thirty and beyond by simply referring to more articles and studies. **The problem with this approach is that when everything and everyone is responsible, then nothing and no-one is.** What is immediately obvious, however, is that **there is no consensus among social scientists (or officials, police officers or politicians) about the causes of vandalism**. Later in this chapter, I will briefly introduce Clarke's framework which groups together different types of variables in an attempt to explain acts of vandalism; but, for the present, I wish to discuss four of the explanations which have either received most notice or deserve more prominence and then I shall pay some attention to the views of young people themselves.

1. FINANCIAL GAIN

For example, professional gangs of adult thieves vandalised phone-boxes as they moved down the coast of South Australia (Wilson, 1990). It has become increasingly recognised (eg Gladstone, 1978, p 25; Giller, 1988) that some acts of vandalism (breaking into a slot machine, or, as happens so frequently now, smashing the windows of cars, or stripping lead from a building) are economically motivated and that such vandalism is incidental ie a means to a financial goal. But, emphatically, most vandalism is not of this kind and is best characterised as "consisting of innumerable incidents of rather petty damage" (Clarke, 1978, p 69) and therefore other explanations are needed.

2. PEER GROUP PRESSURE

"...the motive for much adolescent vandalism is a boy's desire to maintain or enhance his status among his peers" (Gladstone, 1978, p 26). But not all adolescent groups promote vandalism. Gladstone (1978, p 34) found that "Long hours on the street in the company of a 'tough' group, lax parenting and negative experiences at school all appear to increase the probability that a boy will become involved in vandalism". For Andrew Wade (1967, p 95), who interviewed 50 young convicted male vandals aged 13 to 17 in Kansas City, Missouri, "...much property destruction by juveniles is a spontaneous outgrowth of group interaction...". Wade's argument is that, because nearly all (male) teenagers are anxious to behave in the ways their peers expect them to, very few are able to refuse a dare to commit an act of vandalism in case their courage or masculinity is impugned by the very group which can offer them status and recognition. "The adolescent will thus participate in acts of property destruction in order not to appear 'chicken'" (Wade, 1967, p 108). Gladstone (1978, p 26) adds an interesting twist to the argument. **In contrast to fist fights which produce as many losers as winners, "...vandalism may be attractive not only because it provides a 'game' in which a boy can prove his manhood but also because this 'game' is one at which every boy can succeed".**

There are three problems with this approach: first, it is clearly an explanation of male behaviour and may have little to say about the motivation of the growing numbers of young female vandals. Pollard (1988, p 23), for example, in his survey of attitudes to vandalism among 2,371 13-16 year-olds in Northumberland, found that the average participation rate for boys was 76%, compared with 54% for girls, whose involvement increased rapidly from 46% at age 13 to 58% at age 14 (see Figure 5.1).

Figure 5.1

Percentage of resondents admitting to having been a vandal

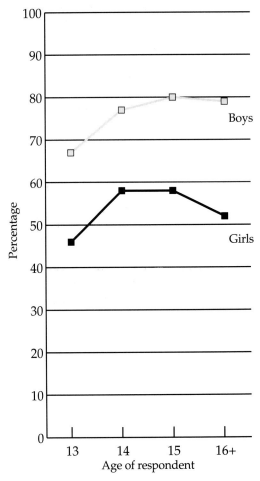

Source: Pollard, Dennis (1988) *Attitudes to Vandalism: A Survey of 13-16 year-olds*, Northumbria Police

Second, I found no incidence in the literature of a young person who was prepared to admit that he or she had been led astray by peer pressure which invariably seem to affect other, weaker members of the group. Glasser and Loughlin (1988, p 153), in a study of adolescent drug taking in a medium-sized American city, seem alone in pointing to "The fact that peer pressure can aid adolescents in <u>controlling</u> or <u>abandoning</u> deviant activities..." (emphasis as in original). Their argument, being novel, well-expressed and convincing (at least, to me), is worth quoting at greater length than normal. For instance, they propose that **adolescent peer groups are "anti-boredom committees"** and that (p 177)

> *...the notion of peer pressure, for all its intuitive appeal and widespread use, is largely a way of negatively stereotyping adolescents. (Peer pressure explanations for adult behaviour are seldom heard.) The idea of peer pressure reveals more about the position of adolescents in society than about the behaviour of adolescents. Much as adolescents are called upon to be both dependent and independent, they are castigated for behaving like other adolescents <u>and</u> criticised if they do <u>not</u> behave that way. In the former case they are seen as falling for peer pressure, in the latter as social misfits or inadequates. (Emphasis as in original)*

Glasser and Loughlin are keen to retain the kernel of truth in explanations based on peer pressure which, to them, is **the over-riding importance of friendship** to their informants; who in fact viewed school "...primarily as a place to socialize with friends" (p 265).

Third, although destroying property appears to be carried out mainly in groups (Hindelang, 1976), peer group pressure will obviously not explain the behaviour of those graffiti artists or vandals who operate on their own. In Pollard's (1988, p 68) survey of 13-16 year-olds, around 16% claimed to act as soloists; and in Gladstone's study (1978, p 27), 19% of those boys reporting high involvement in vandalism were seldom or never in a group. Hindelang (1976, p 123) concluded "...that relying solely on officially recorded delinquent events has led researchers and theorists to over-emphasize the extent to which delinquencies are committed in groups". The fact is, however, that we know next to nothing about the solitary delinquent or vandal.

3. PLEASURE

Zimbardo (1973, p 89) abandoned cars in New York and on the Stanford University campus to observe how they were vandalised and by whom. Within ten minutes the car in New York had been stripped of all usable parts and within a day it had been randomly but comprehensively smashed by a steady stream of vandals. A week passed on the campus of Stanford

University without the abandoned car being attacked and so Zimbardo and his graduate students decided to take a sledge hammer to the car themselves to see if others would then follow suit: "Although everyone knew that the sequence was being filmed, the students got 'carried away' temporarily. Once one person had begun to wield the sledge hammer, it was difficult to get him to stop and pass it to the next pair of eager hands. Finally, they all acted simultaneously...They later reported that feeling the metal or glass give way under the force of their blows was stimulating and pleasurable."

Allen (1984) has elevated the sheer pleasure experienced in destroying objects into "the aesthetic theory of vandalism", which has two distinctive features according to him. First, the emphasis is on factors intrinsic to the stimulus itself and the particular context rather than on individual personality traits. Second, the psychological processes underlying acts of pleasurable vandalism are considered to be normal and universal rather than pathological and specific to convicted vandals. He is right to stress the social drama of having "a big night out on the town" at weekends, when young people report "...in connection with their vandalism, that it was great fun trying to avoid getting caught and running away from the police and other adults. The risk and danger, the uncertainty, the thrill of evasive action, are all arousing and hence enjoyable" (Allen, 1984, p 79).

He goes further by arguing that "...destruction can be an aesthetic experience: breaking can be beautiful...Artists as well as psychologists have noted that a close affinity exists between art and destruction - or more generally between creative and destructive acts" (Ibid, p 88). The smashing of guitars on stage by pop stars still tends to be reported as a bizarre or mindless act but Allen's line of reasoning would connect such behaviour to a long line of painters, sculptors and musicians who have insisted on presenting their acts of destruction as art and who have simultaneously derived pleasure from scandalising the bourgeoisie (for details, see Allen, 1984, pp 80-82). Nor are such ideas a recent development in western thinking; Michael Bakunin produced his famous phrase "The urge to destroy is also a creative urge" in 1842. Ellerby (1966, p 65) sought to extend this argument but his questions are rather loaded: "Is destruction always negative and construction always creative" and is vandalism "...an imperfect form of creativity"?

4. MANUFACTURED MALICE AND EXCITEMENT AS A SOLUTION

The enduring strength of Stan Cohen's original argument in 1973 is that **he connected the fun, the pleasure and the malice to be had from criminal damage with the structural roots of the problem** in order to explain why the most prevalent form of vandalism is committed by working-class offenders. And there is a continuing need to do justice to both sides of the argument. The evidence he drew on to support his case is understandable rather than dated now and the new structural conditions, within which young people grow up and try to make a life for themselves, need to be briefly depicted.

Let us begin with their experiences at school. David Hargreaves (1982, p 17) takes an uncompromising view: "...our present secondary school system...exerts on many pupils, particularly but by no means exclusively from the working-class, a destruction of their dignity which is so massive and pervasive that few subsequently recover from it". It is therefore no surprise that 40% of all pupils still leave school at the earliest possible moment and are then confronted <u>either</u> with dead-end jobs without training or prospects, <u>or</u> Youth Training for two years on schemes which have been shown to be highly variable in quality (Lee et al, 1990) and to be reinforcing sex inequalities (Cockburn, 1987) <u>or</u> unemployment. Sooner rather than later, they all learn their place in society but a section find their opportunities for useful, well-paid jobs, for further education and training and private housing either blocked or non-existent. Pahl (1984, pp 313-4) has described a growing process of **polarisation within the working-class**, "...with households busily engaged in all forms of work at one pole and households unable to do a wide range of work at the other...The division between the more affluent home-owning households of ordinary working people and the less advantaged underclass households is coming to be more significant than conventional divisions based on the manual/non-manual distinction".

Others, like Ashton et al (1987, p 211) point to the increasing introduction by firms of **employment practices which distinguish between core and peripheral workers**: "Core members with relatively well-paid and secure employment were expected to be flexible, multi-skilled and experienced. There was a trend towards using part-time and temporary labour in peripheral jobs. Married women were normally preferred in part-time employment". What seems to be happening is that large numbers of young people and adults are being confined to a segment of the labour market characterised by low paid, insecure and casual jobs or government schemes or recurrent unemployment which becomes steadily longer in duration.

In recent years Ralf Dahrendorf has been developing the theme of "the underclass and the future of Britain". His central argument can be summarised as follows: the underclass is a cancer that eats away at the texture of societies. He is not saying that the underclass itself is sick or to be held responsible for its own condition. The point is rather that the underclass has an effect on the rest of society. In his own words **"if a sizeable portion of the young have no stake in a society, then society itself appears to have given up its stake in the future"**. And again, "The existence of an underclass violates the fundamental assumption of modern, free societies which is that everyone without exception is a citizen with certain entitlements common to all" (1987, p 10).

One of the symptoms he points to is the rise in football hooliganism:

> ...the old working-class game of football has become in some places, an underclass game, with significant consequences for attendance figures, but above all for the kind of people who go and the incidents which one has to prepare for, if one goes. The cattle trains taking 'fans' to and from games are a shocking testimony to our inability to create a society of citizens with all the rights and responsibilities that go with the status (1987, p 5).

The existence of an underclass is not only objectionable on moral grounds; it also threatens the social and political stability of Britain and other western countries. Nor is the existence of an underclass a temporary aberration or a statistical blip, as Ray Gosling pointed out in his recent Channel 4 programme *Class by Class*, but the direct outcome of a system where individual is pitted against individual and where individual achievement is accorded the highest value. The corollary for any society organised along these Darwinian lines, "...is individual failure and consciousness of failure", as Richard Titmuss (1958, p 55) pointed out over thirty years ago.

Dahrendorf also listed the factors associated with the emergence of this new class and they are highly predictable: unemployment, low income, poor educational qualifications, illiteracy, teenage pregnancies, slum housing, inner-city blight and racial prejudice. Among the symptoms of underclass behaviour he brackets football hooliganism with the riots which broke out in 1981. These, he warns, have not been forgotten and may indeed recur, as in fact they did in different ways in Cardiff, Birmingham, Oxford and the North East of England in the late summer of 1991:

> *...they are not the beginning of a new great social movement - to be compared with some of the incidents which accompanied the formation of the labour movement in the nineteenth century - but situational expressions of a frustration which can go on and on and on (1987, p 5).*

Whatever the terminology used, whether polarisation by Pahl, core/ periphery structures by Ashton and his colleagues, or an underclass by Dahrendorf, it is clear that the last ten years have witnessed some fundamental changes to the nature and culture of work, and to the occupational structure in western societies. Besides, **the cost of restructuring British industry has fallen unequally on the population**, with some regions of the country (the North, the West of Scotland and Wales) and some sections of the community in all regions (young adults, the long-term unemployed and ethnic minorities) becoming more and more marginalised. Projections about changes in the British labour market (eg Lindley, 1987) stress that gains in managerial and administrative posts will be offset in the next ten years by a further decline (of about 600,000) in labouring and unskilled jobs. Industry's growing need for ever higher levels of general education and vocational training from its workers may leave large sections of the community, whose experiences of schooling appear to have put them off education for the foreseeable future, permanently out of employment or in sub-employment.

There are strict limits to the power of empathy. What must it feel like to come slowly to the realisation at the ages of fourteen or sixteen that you, your family, your neighbours and perhaps your whole community are "surplus to requirements", as I once heard an MSC official describe the long-term unemployed in the North East of England? The sense of powerlessness, the drabness of the housing estate, the deteriorating fabric of the local schools and the poverty of body and spirit brought about by 'shit' jobs, 'govvie' schemes and unemployment, all combine to leave young people 'on the edge of desperation'. **As a solution to the problems society has created for them, vandalism is just right - this is the essence of Cohen's argument.** In his own words "It is satisfying and provides just the right amount of risk. If one is looking for toughness, excitement, action and a sense of control (however self-defeating and illusory in the long run), then school and work do not provide the right arenas" (1973a, p 53). Vandalism allows "the lads" (and perhaps also "the lasses") to be deliberately provoking, to raise two fingers to the system which has so undermined their self-respect and left them without a future. The torn conveyor belt, broken street lamps and smashed schools are then best understood as "...statements made by people who have few other opportunities for self-expression" (Laurie Taylor, 1973, p 63).

There is one argument which needs to be added, concerning the changing pattern of young people's drinking. The decline in cinema and dance-hall attendance and the growth of pubs designed specifically to cater for affluent youth have combined to alter their social behaviour. As Mary Tuck (1989, p 66) wrote in her study of *Drinking and Disorder*:

> *Going out to the pub is quite simply what young people do on a weekend evening, to meet others and to enjoy themselves...Young people leave pubs en masse at the same hour, emerge on the streets still looking for further entertainment, cluster at fast-food outlets or at other gathering points and are at this point excitable tinder, ready for any spark which may cause quarrels or violence.*

Or, I would add, vandalism.

But the changes go deeper than this. **Young people's drinking practices can only be understood as part of their cultural response to the changing economic context within which they create a social life for themselves.** As Les Gofton (1990) has graphically described, the leisure drinking of the young is now differently <u>organised</u>. A major break has been made away from the traditional pattern of hard drinking among working-class men, which celebrated masculinity, hard physical labour and being sociable with your work mates or neighbours. Over the last ten years, a new pattern has come to be established. In Gofton's words (1990, p 36):

> *The layout and decor of bars have changed as have the products they sell and the entertainment which brings in the trade (music, live and canned, lightshows, quizzes and cabaret). Pubs have changed because of the market power of the young.*

In the North East, for example, young men and women on Friday and Saturday nights will stay in a pub only as long as it takes to consume their first drink and then move on to the next pub on the circuit; they are prepared to queue and even to pay entrance charges to gain admittance to the most fashionable places, practices which frankly astonish the traditional, working-class adult drinker.

These changes have raised a number of issues which we, the adult community, seem loath to confront. First, **the centres of most cities and towns are virtually surrendered to the young on Friday and Saturday evenings.** Middle-aged people who happen to be out on the town at weekends turn a blind eye towards the display behaviour of young adults and hope to scuttle past without being noticed.

Second, **under-age drinking is now endemic in this country**, in rural as well as inner-city or suburban areas and the law in this respect is being widely and openly disregarded. Careful studies by the Home Office Research Unit have in recent years established, for example, that "...in Guildford and Woking one third of the young men aged 16-17 were using pubs at the weekend" (Tuck, 1989, p 69) and that "...under-age drinkers are more likely than older ones to be involved in disorder" (Tuck, 1989, p 68). Third, evidence has been mounting for some time (Dorn, 1983; Coffield et al, 1986) that many young adults, females as well as males, are regularly drinking to excess; they set out with the deliberate intention of getting 'smashed' or 'paralytic', and are highly resistant to any health education campaigns or advertisements which stress sensible drinking.

The above has not been written by a teetotal Calvinistic Scot who is seeking to deny young adults pleasures which he himself enjoys; nor am I trying to create a moral panic over teenage drunkenness. Rather, I am trying to suggest calmly but firmly that markedly different and potentially dangerous patterns (dangerous, that is, to the health of some of these young people) are being developed which need a response from the community as a whole and some tentative proposals are made in the final chapter.

THE VIEWS OF YOUNG PEOPLE

Dennis Pollard (1988, p 41) asked his 13-16 year-olds to tick, from a pre-determined list of seventeen "causes of vandalism", those they thought were the most important. Although he acknowledges that open-ended interviews would have been a preferable method of eliciting the

Table 5.1

Percentage choosing as very important causes of vandalism

% citing from list as "very important" cause

Glue sniffing	55%
Unemployment	44%
Nothing for young people to do	43%
Not much control by parents	43%
Punishment not hard enough	43%
Drinking	37%
To steal something	36%
Not bothered about public buildings	32%
Not bothered if caught	32%
For a laugh with friends	31%
No one has an interest in them	29%
Area already run down	27%
Not bothered about other's property	26%
Copying what others do	23%
Violence on TV/video	22%
Not much control by schools	21%
Get own back on world	19%

Source: Pollard, Dennis (1988) *Attitudes to Vandalism: A Survey of 13-16 year-olds,* Northumbria Police

uninfluenced ideas of his respondents, the results, presented in Table 5.1, are still of interest. There were clear differences between the answers of self-confessed 'vandals' and 'non-vandals', with the former giving higher than average ratings as "very important causes" to "Nothing for young people to do", "Area already run down" and "Unemployment". When his informants were invited to add any comments they wanted, the most frequent response was "Nothing much for young people to do" and Pollard concluded "...many pleas were made bemoaning the lot of young people for whom desired facilities were far away, too expensive, barred to them or not provided" (Ibid, p 42). The second most frequent spontaneous comment was "To prove you're not chicken" or "To keep in with friends". So this survey lends support to both Cohen's thesis and the importance to teenagers of meeting the expectations of their group.

CLARKE'S MODEL

Ron Clarke (1977 and 1980) has brought together into one framework, here presented in Figure 5.2, the most common theories drawn from biology, psychology and sociology to explain acts of vandalism. Heredity (Group 2 in the diagram) is the favoured explanation of biologists, while psychologists tend to stress child-rearing practices and the personality of the offender (Groups 1 and 3). Sociologists, on the other hand, typically emphasise social status and environmental factors (Groups 4 and 5). Over the last fifteen years, criminologists have increasingly drawn attention to 'situational factors' (Groups 6 and 7), in the belief that people's behaviour is influenced more by the particular context in which they find themselves than by their personality or social origins. Baker and Waddon (1989) claim to have adapted and extended Clarke's original 1977 model, but they have in fact simply substituted "peer group influence" for "crises and events" (Group 6).

The prime value of the approach is its comprehensiveness in pulling together such disparate and competing ideas into one model. Attempts to understand a particular incident of criminal damage will, however, still need to draw on different combinations of factors with different emphases being attached to those variables considered to be most implicated in the offence. An improvement to the system would be, however, a more openly sociological interpretation of the factors contained in Group 8; what we need are the full accounts given by individuals for their conduct and their rationalisations of it. Stan Cohen explains the significance of this strategy: "...the function of these statements is seen as repairing social bonds: bringing the actor back into line with a group whose norms have been violated" (1984a, p 57). The motives advanced by culprits are not infinite or endlessly subjective, but are socially patterned and repetitive; **in this way links are forged between the explanations of individuals and social structure.**

A second advantage is that Clarke's model pays considerably more attention than previous theorists to situational factors in the explanation of vandalism;

this emphasis also has an important practical implication for it argues that vandalism may best be prevented by manipulating opportunities for crime rather than modifying the personality or home background of offenders. But that is the subject of Chapter 9 on prevention.

Figure 5.2

Explanations of vandalism

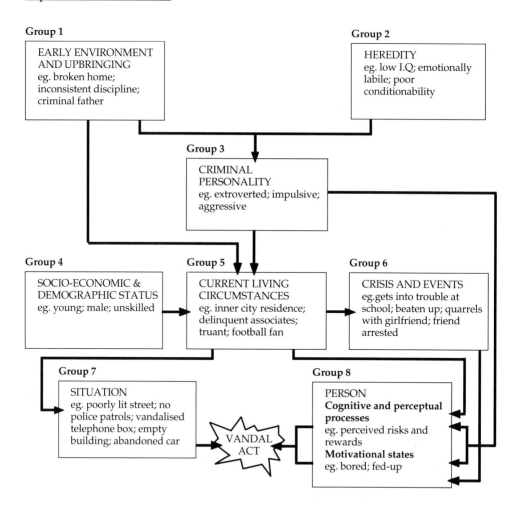

Source: Clarke, RVG and Mayhew, P (1980) *Designing Out Crime*, London: HMSO, p 4

CHAPTER 6

GRAFFITI - URBAN SCOURGE OR FOLK ART?

Is graffiti "the scourge of the urban environment", as *Crime Prevention News* (Summer, 1989) dubs it, or is it a colourful, vibrant folk art, as Norman Mailer (1974) would have us believe? As ever, the battle-lines are drawn up on either side of a chasm filled with mutual suspicion and misunderstandings. I propose to investigate both sides of the argument before ending the chapter with a brief account of how New York, which in the 1970s became the home of a new genre created by graffiti writers using spray cans, cleaned up its subway trains and managed to keep them clean.

Anyone, however, who travels the length or breadth of contemporary Britain by car, bus or train cannot fail to see bus shelters, under-passes, factory walls, shop fronts and especially public buildings covered in either infantile scribbles or elaborate, stylised, multi-coloured writing. My own response is mixed. I have visited public parks where the obscenities and the racist slogans on boards and walls have transformed a peaceful and relaxing environment into a place of intolerance, imminent violence and social distress. On the other hand, the colour, humour and vibrancy of some graffiti art have successfully titivated some dark and ugly corners on my walks to and from railway stations and car parks. **A clear distinction ought to be made between these two types of graffiti but it rarely is.**

Wallace and Whitehead (1989, p 9) offer a definition of graffiti as "...unwanted painting, writing, gouging or scratching on walls or other surfaces". But such restraint is unusual where this topic is concerned; the writing on the wall has provoked some purple passages both in support and in condemnation, as we shall see.

For some, graffiti soon became "...the premier symbol of the failure of government to protect citizens from the depradations of vandals and criminals" (Sloan-Howitt and Kelling, 1990, p 131). For Mayor Lindsay and his administration in New York, graffiti was the "thoughtless and irresponsible behaviour" of "graffiti pigs" and "insecure cowards", and his theory was "...that the rash of graffiti madness was related to mental health problems" (all quoted by Mailer, 1974). The mood of the city authorities in the early 1970s was caught in the phase "Filth is sprouting on the walls" and the impact on the inhabitants, according to their Mayor, was "...profoundly depressing - it truly hurt people's moods. The life would go out of everybody when they saw the cars defaced, they saw it as defacement, no question of that. And we kept hearing one request over and over, 'Can't you do something about it?'" (Mailer, 1974).

The colour, humour and vibrancy of some graffiti art can successfully titivate some dark ugly corners...

But the New Yorker's question raises in acute form <u>the</u> problem with unwanted graffiti: it is highly visible, it is a damned nuisance and an expense to those in authority, it is "...sensitive (in the sense of immediately registering urban decay..." (Cohen, 1984a, p 58), and yet it is "...not serious enough to be accorded top priority..." (Ekblom, 1989, p 17) by the police or other authority figures.

Glazer (quoted by Sloan-Howitt and Kelling, 1990, p 132) neatly summed up the dilemma:

> *Graffiti raise the odd problem of a crime that is, compared to others, relatively trivial but whose aggregate effects on the environment of millions of people are massive. In the New York situation especially, it contributes to a prevailing sense of the incapacity of government, and the uncontrollability of youthful criminal behaviour, and a resultant uneasiness and fear. Minor infractions aggregate into something that reaches and affects every subway passenger.*

Norman Mailer was one of the first to come to the defence of the graffiti artists, but his overblown and florid style may well have alienated many potential sympathisers. He argued that, far from scribbling obscenities of the kind to be found on toilet walls throughout the States, the youngsters were in fact writing adaptations of their own names in a highly stylised way which had blossomed into a well-defined sub-culture with its own distinctive vocabulary and hierarchy. In his own inimitable words:

> *What a quintessential marriage of cool and style to write your name in giant separate living letters, large as animals, lithe as snakes, mysterious as Arabic and Chinese curls of alphabet, and to do it in the heat of a winter night when the hands are frozen and only the heart is hot with fear (Mailer, 1974).*

In a publication emblazoned with huge, colour photographs of hundreds of the names with which New York had been 'hit', Mailer interviewed a number of the leading graffiti writers who claimed that they won prestige, recognition and status from "hitting" four or five times a day and then "watching My Name Go By" through "the monumental drabs of South Bronx". One of them even ventured to claim that writing the Name "...is the <u>faith</u> of graffiti" (Mailer, 1974, emphasis as in original).

But such proper appreciation by Mailer of the deviants' story soon fell into the trap of romanticising their artistic output and their suffering. When describing, for instance, how those who were caught were obliged to clean the subway cars and so erase the work of others, he commented: "All proportions kept, it may be in simple pain of heart have been not altogether unequal to condemning Cézanne to wipe out the works of Van Gogh" (Mailer, 1974). **Mailer,** I suggest, **would not recognise a due sense of proportion even if he fell over one in the street**. What cannot be contested is that some of the graffiti 'masters' began selling their works for between 200 and 3,000 dollars a time in the mid 1970s.

Since then, graffiti art has come into its own with magazines, exhibitions and photo-books like Martha Cooper and Henry Chalfont's *Subway Art* being dedicated to the cult in the States and similar collections (eg Heyne, 1987) in Germany. Cooper and Chalfont stalked trains through the labyrinth of New York's transit system to record in photos hundreds of paintings that no longer exist. They emphasise how much preparation went into the creation of these elaborate graffiti, with writers choosing characters, themes, style (bubble or straight letters or wildstyle) and colours in their "piece book" (or sketchbook). A "top-to-bottom" piece which covered the whole of the subway car could take eight hours to complete and require twenty cans of spray paint. The writers were usually boys of high school age but there were also girl members of the "crews" which gave themselves such names as

"United Artists" or OTB ("Out Ta Bomb"). In the 1960s gang members had written their names up in the streets to mark out their territory but such crude graffiti developed into "...a highly sophisticated calligraphy that flowers in a constantly changing, bold and brilliant travelling show on the city's subway system" (Cooper and Chalfont, 1984, p 90). Gregory Wright (personal communication) in California has also developed an ingenious technique of "reprocessing" graffiti, whereby public eyesores are worked on, fleshed out and completed so that they bring colour and pleasure to the community. Young Chicano 'muralistas' have been employed so successfully for this task that they have gone on to sell the pattern to cloth and textile manufacturers, and to the designers of shirts, wallpaper and tiles.

What purposes are served by such publications as Heyne's which tend to sanitise and emasculate the originals? Their immediate, stated aim is to celebrate the work of graffiti artists but I would like to suggest that they perform another function: they help the comfortable middle-class learn to live with - and make light of - obvious symptoms of social distress. For example, the gents toilet in Prince's Square (the beautiful, new shopping arcade in Glasgow) even sports graffiti tiles which carry such aphorisms as "Patience is a Virtue", followed by "I knew Patience before she became a Virtue". There are, I admit, far more witty graffiti and Nigel Rees (1982) has produced a series of paperback collections of them.

Throughout Britain, Weetabix adverts began to feature graffiti and Charles Saatchi brought 'pieces' from New York graffiti artists. In May 1989 the London Union of Youth Clubs staged an exhibition, workshop, and a seminar on 'Graffiti Art' at the South London Art Gallery in order "...to provide a more informed and positive response by the authorities and to limit the danger to those young people who risk death and criminalisation in their attempts to express their creativity illegally" (David Holloway, 1989, p 2). It was a considerable advance to have discussions between graffiti artists and representatives of the police, British Railway Transport Police and London Transport; and exhibiting the artists' work, which **they preferred to be called 'Aerosol Art' or 'Spray Can Art' rather than graffiti**, resulted in many of the 'pieces' being sold. On the other hand there is no evidence from the report of the seminar (Roberts, 1990) that the entrenched views of the authorities, which tended to write off completely the creativity shown by young people, were even dented. Some of the positive outcomes were: the consensus that there were three basic types of graffiti (a 'piece', a 'tag' usually made with a marker pen, and obscene scribbles) and all the artists publicly disowned the third category; the plea by young people that the first type was an art form, that it should be recognised as such and that all young adults needed some space within which to explore and develop their abilities.

A fascinating example of co-operation betwen the authorities and graffitists was given by a group called 'Beyond Graffiti' from Southampton: "A previously vandalized, graffiti daubed multi-storey car park that was intimidating to car users was effectively transformed by the Services Department consulting with graffiti artists/projects and asked them to design and then decorate the car park with the approved designs" (Roberts, 1990, p 4). This diversion of young people's creativity into legitimate channels has apparently resulted in reduced levels of crime and a better atmosphere between the community at large and youth in the city; such success stories need to be properly evaluated, publicised and introduced elsewhere.

The clear aim of the graffiti writers is to make their art form more socially acceptable and perhaps even to decriminalise both the activity and the artists. **What is not so well understood by adults is the close connection between graffiti art and youth culture.** In Spring 1990, for example, graffiti artists joined dancers and three rock bands for a ten day tour of Ireland; and an Italian publishing house invited five 'spray can stylists' or 'graff-ites' to make a week-long tour of Europe to display their skills. They found much more acceptance of their work in Milan and Amsterdam than in London and even met 'graff-ites' from London who were working in Paris and were funded by French arts councils (see Rose, 1990).

The specialised vocabulary clearly differentiates between the different types of graffiti - to 'tag' is to add your highly stylised signature, while to 'piece' (from 'masterpiece') is to create a complete picture. Trains which have been 'tagged' or 'pieced' are said to have been 'bombed' or 'hit' in this country, and 'bombed' or 'killed' in the States. Those who know how to yield the 'bunts' (from cans of Bunt-Lac spray) are 'writers' who 'burn' or beat the competition with 'def' (ie really good, derived from death) designs, while those still learning are 'scribblers' or 'toys' whose 'throw-ups' (quickly painted outlines) are 'wak' (substandard, inept, with drips visible). According to Pete May (1989, p 7), "dogging" is "...where you write over other people's work". A full list of specialist terms can be found in Cooper and Chalfont (1984, p 27).

In January 1991, an 18 year-old art student from Blackpool was banned by magistrates from every railway bridge in Britain after he pleaded guilty to seven charges of criminal damage using spray cans. His explanation deserves to be given in full; notice how he attempts to avoid censure by refusing to accept the label of vandal:

> It's a good feeling - like being an outlaw. Out there in the night with a couple of friends on your own. You're creating something wonderful and beautiful for others to enjoy. I understand that British Rail don't want to see murals on their walls, but I don't look upon it as vandalism. It's a popular art. Unfortunately a majority of people are ill-informed and don't understand what the culture is about. It's all about self-expression. We are adding something colourful to a bland, blank surface which others will see and admire. It may not be fully appreciated at the moment, but in due course I believe it will be recognised as an art form (The Guardian, 21 January, 1991).

The scale of the task faced by British Rail and other transport authorities is brought home by such a fluent and confident self-justification from someone claiming to be a member of a misunderstood cult. Not even the widespread publicity given to two tragic deaths (of a teenage boy who was trying to spray a moving train at Kilburn underground station or of another graffiti artist who was killed on a railway line while being chased by British Railway Transport Police) appears to have acted as a deterrent; in all, since 1987 five teenagers have been killed while daubing slogans on trains (The Times, 24 August, 1991). On the contrary, if graffiti writing is "a fame game for kids" (May, 1989, p 8), then the reputation of the successful writers is likely to be enhanced all the more if the activity becomes fraught with danger.

The motives which sustain this behaviour, however, go beyond the central aim of achieving a reputation by getting one's 'tag' up and having it seen across the city; there are also risks and excitements to enjoy, the pleasure of hearing your 'pieces' being discussed by other passengers, the comradeship of, and competition against, other 'crew' members, the fun of outwitting guards or policemen and the satisfaction to be had from developing your own creativity and artistic style. In addition, Ekblom (1988, p 18) interviewed 12 convicted offenders and 20 other active graffitists who explained that "Train sides are physically good canvasses - large slabs of smooth, plain aluminium" and that "Paint spray cans are ideal tools - they are clean, portable, convenient and readily obtainable".

Faced with such determined youngsters who can arm themselves so easily with the requisite tools, how was it that the New York City Transit Authority rendered all 6,000 of its subway cars free of graffiti within five years? Their strategy consisted of three key elements. First, measures were chosen which were based on an understanding of the phenomenon: the motivation which was thought to lie at the heart of graffiti writing was attacked by depriving youths of the satisfaction of having their work seen: "All graffiti was to be removed within 2 hours or the car would be pulled from service. Police were assigned to ride these trains full-time while they were in service" (Sloan-Howitt and Kelling, 1990, p 133). Second, management set all parts of the system attainable and challenging goals and provided the resources necessary to meet them. The clean car programme began modestly with two trains and expanded slowly as real successes were achieved. Third, all the organisations involved (police, train depots, drivers, cleaners etc) were co-ordinated and their success rate monitored regularly. In the end, nothing succeeded like success and "a seemingly intractable problem", which Mailer at one point thought would take over the world, was apparently solved.

Back in Britain, Colin Ward (1990, p 8) has asked the appropriate question: how is it that graffitists can have such long uninterrupted access to sites or railway rolling-stock to create such elaborate 'pieces'? He answers his own question thus: "...staff-cutting exercises in the interests of economy have ensured that often no-one is exercising any supervisory function in, for example, unmanned railway stations". (I cannot resist quoting (from May 1989, p 8) the message to graffiti writers left by London Transport cleaners which read "Merry Christmas and thanks for the overtime".) If we want to emulate the "spectacular success" (Sloan-Howitt and Kelling, 1990, p 136) of New York city, then **a campaign based on interdepartmental co-ordination, specific goals, strong leadership and sufficient resources will be necessary**. One caveat. May (1989, p 9) reports that the graffiti in New York have not disappeared entirely but rather have been displaced from the subway to garbage trucks: "A huge white garbage truck is a nice ripe target".

CHAPTER 7

ATTACKS ON DEFENSIBLE SPACE

According to Oscar Newman (1980, p 8), the suburbs of American cities have become "...upper-income, economically pure, racially intact enclaves. They provide segregation at the grand scale". The inner-city areas of our own large metropolitan cities have for some time been following the pattern which was established earlier in the States, but we seem incapable of learning from their experiences. Again, in Newman's words (1980, p 5):

> We now content ourselves with the safe fortresses of white, middle-class suburbia. American society has become polarised into suburban, white, and wealthy versus urban, dark, and poor. The middle-class has put tens of miles between themselves and their fears and have forsaken the environments which once provided them with the nourishment essential to their own development. They have left behind the decaying remnants of a once rich urban environment to shelter the last generation of urban migrants.

Newman argued fiercely against this withdrawal of the wealthy into security-guarded fortresses for three reasons. First, what began as an evasion of the problem of crime soon develops into a retreat into indifference. Second, "when people begin to protect themselves as individuals and not as a community, the battle against crime is effectively lost" (1972, p 3). Finally, the physical design of our cities deteriorates because the housing complexes of the rich become walled-off from their surrounding neighbourhoods.

Whatever we may think of his research methods and of his polemical style (and there have been fierce criticisms of both), we also need to acknowledge that from the publication of his first book *Defensible Space* in 1972, **Oscar Newman has drawn attention to a major but neglected theme, namely how crime can be prevented through architectural design**. His fundamental proposition was that crime could be reduced through "...restructuring the residential environments of our cities so they can again become livable and controlled, controlled not by police but by a community of people sharing a common terrain" (1972, p 2). He argued that if residents could be given back a sense of pride in, and of belonging to, their immediate environment, then their feelings of responsibility for that environment and their wish to protect it would be increased.

A theory can in part be judged by the amount of creative research it stimulates and, by this criterion, Newman's work has proved fruitful. Two studies conducted in this country are briefly reviewed in order to give an indication of the strengths and weaknesses of Newman's ideas - Sheena Wilson's (1980) research into vandalism and defensible space on London housing estates and also the report by Mayhew et al (1980b) into whether the vandalism to telephone kiosks is influenced by the amount of "natural" surveillance they receive from members of the public.

Wilson examined the rates of vandalism in 285 separate blocks of dwellings on 38 inner London public housing estates in order to test the relationship between vandalism and "defensible space". Her findings were mixed. The author concluded by suggesting that the principles of defensible space should be incorporated into the future design of housing estates (public areas such as entrances were much more vandalised, as Newman predicted), but "...child density emerged as the single most important variable of those studied" (1980, p 61).

Newman had also hypothesised (1972, p 80) that design could also improve the ability of residents to observe the public areas in their housing projects (or, as we would say, 'estates'); such changes would deter crime, lessen the anxiety of inhabitants and create an overall image of a safe environment. Mayhew et al set out to study the impact of such "natural" surveillance on vandalism to 217 telephone kiosks in the London Borough of Greenwich. The results suggested that

> ...kiosk vandalism is more strongly related to certain characteristics of the population living near individual kiosks than to physical factors pertaining to their siting, and in this respect they are consistent with Newman's later (1976) work which showed that the social make-up of local housing estate inhabitants contributed more to levels of crime and vandalism than housing design (Mayhew et al, 1980b, p 73).

Both the studies I have referred to are very much in line with the general findings from research into defensible space in this country and in the States and that indeed was a factor in their selection.

A number of highly critical reviews of *Defensible Space* were published (see Bottoms, 1974; Mawby, 1977; and Mayhew, 1979, for instance), wherein Newman was accused of "architectural determinism", "rather amateurish use of research techniques, masked by a presentation which favours political oratory rather than scientific examination" and the neglect of other factors apart from design in the creation of crime. Those who have attempted an overall evaluation of his contribution have emphasised the debt we all owe him for drawing attention to the important relationship between design and crime and have admitted that his later work in 1976 and 1980 responded to most of the criticisms which were initially made of *Defensible Space*. Mayhew's (1979, p 156) careful review of all the research studies inspired by Newman does

> *...not suggest that judicious architecture is the key to a crime-free environment. Rather, they indicate that design has to compete with a number of other factors crucial amongst which may be residents' willingness to participate in running their environment, and the quality of outside management. If not more important may be the types of resident families, in particular the number of offenders living in the vicinity and the ratio of children to adults.*

The reawakening of interest in the quality of public housing, which was brought about in part by Newman, put the spotlight back on the disproportionate levels of crime suffered by large, difficult-to-let council estates on the outskirts of so many British cities. Anne Power (1989) has listed the characteristics of these run-down estates: they have bad reputations which residents try to escape from and others struggle to avoid; they tend to be built on a large scale, are communal in their design with many unguarded, exposed and unused areas of the kind Newman emphasised, and by their scale and monotony they are marked-off, marooned, and separate from other housing areas.

Furthermore, she criticised Alice Coleman's widely read and provocative study *Utopia on Trial: Vision and Reality in Planned Housing* for assuming that "...people behave badly <u>because</u> of design, rather than that certain designs are unpopular and hard to deal with as a result of which those <u>who have least ability to cope</u> are the most likely to be rehoused in the least popular blocks..." (1989, p 217, emphasis as in original). Alice Coleman (second edition, 1990, p 170) had argued that "problem estates can breed their own anti-social elements, leading to increased delinquency and crime..." and that "...human behaviour tends to deteriorate under the stress of inappropriate habitats". In more detail, she claimed that, as the design of modern public housing estates worsens and blocks of flats become higher, "...litter is joined by graffiti, and then successively by vandal damage, by family breakdown necessitating the placing of children in care, and by excrement" (Ibid). Since her book was first published in 1985, some of her key propositions have been challenged; for instance, Hillier (1986) dismissed her conclusions about children in care because she had not corrected her figures for population size and Ravetz (1988) similarly attacked her claim that the incidence of vandalism rises with the size of the block of flats. Ravetz (1988, p 157) summarized her opposition thus "...it is virtually impossible to demonstrate clear causal connections between design and crime and vandalism". These arguments led Anne Power (1989, p 216) to conclude as follows:

> *The serious crime problem of many unpopular estates of houses outside London would suggest that design is only one of many elements, and by no means the critical determinant. It is far more likely that unpopular design, along with other characteristics causing unpopularity such as the size and reputation of estates, deters would-be applicants and creates a spiral of falling appeal so that only the most desperate and most excluded are prepared to move there.*

One of the individuals who gave evidence to the enquiry set up by the GLC's Police Committee into vandalism in London described his estate as "a vandal's paradise" (1984, p 11). Witnesses articulated their basic right to live without fear of crime, racial harassment and vandalism; and Paul Harrison (1983) has provided us with a disturbing picture of the quality of life for old age pensioners and innocent children on such "dump" estates which are as neglected by the landlords as by the tenants:

Systematic destruction of young trees...

The photographs on this page and opposite where taken by Exit.

Perhaps the most graphic indication of this is the widespread use of public spaces as public toilets. On many estates residents complain not only of dogs, but of passers-through, drunks, children and youths urinating and even excreting on balconies, in lifts and in stair wells.

For families with little choice of where to live, vandalism and graffiti are not the only, or perhaps even the worst, pollutants of their environment. Norman Mailer (1974), after his meeting with Mayor Lindsay, walked off reflecting what he, Mailer, would have done about graffiti if their roles had been reversed: "The answer was simple - nobody like himself would ever be elected Mayor until the people agreed bad architecture was as poisonous as bad food". For people living on 'sink' estates, the quality of the housing, the quality of the food and the quality of the local politicians have all tended to be poor.

CHAPTER 8

TO BLAZES WITH SCHOOL!

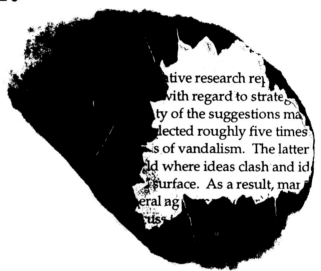

tive research re]
vith regard to strate
ty of the suggestions ma
lected roughly five times
s of vandalism. The latter
ld where ideas clash and id
surface. As a result, mar
eral ag
uss

Malicious damage to school premises appears to be directed at particular regimes and teachers who have attacked the dignity of pupils.

"As a meaningful mode of communication, school vandalism is hard to beat: no other means is so direct, so anonymous, or provides one with such instantaneous results". So write Zwier and Vaughan (1984, p 286), and their conclusion is obviously similar to Stan Cohen's remark that vandalism, more generally, is just right as a solution. Given the fact that most young vandals and arsonists turn their attacks against their own schools, there is not much support in the literature for the idea that school vandalism is 'motiveless', 'mindless' or 'arbitrary'. Indeed, it is difficult to escape the conclusion that, although malicious damage to school premises is widespread, it seems nonetheless to be directed at particular regimes and teachers who have attacked the dignity of pupils who then respond through vandalism.

The work on school vandalism parallels closely the findings we have already described and, as will shortly become clear, suffers from the same kind of problem. The search for <u>the</u> causes of school vandalism has, for instance, proved as fruitless as the attempts to find the reasons for criminal damage or for crime itself. What the research reports have come up with is a list of correlations which are associated with a high incidence of vandalism in schools but which cannot be said to have <u>caused</u> the damage. Such a list would include: teacher apathy, low achievement and dislike of school (by pupils, that is), a lack of interest in the school by the local community, a high turnover of teachers, and even the age of the head teacher (with more vandalism in the schools run by older heads).

Gladstone (1978, p 32) in his study of vandalism amongst adolescent schoolboys, was able to show that "...a negative attitude to school would appear to be associated with vandalism regardless of academic success or failure" and this finding has important implications for prevention in that, although failure seems to be endemic in our educational system, "...dislike of school would seem, at least in principle, less inevitable even among boys who make little headway with academic studies" (p 37).

This suggestion concerning the quality of education deserves to be kept in mind when recommendations are being considered, but for the present there is merit in examining in more detail a study such as Nathan Goldman's (1961) which set out to discover what factors distinguish schools which suffer high damage from those with little. After interviewing 367 teachers and 1,170 pupils from 16 schools in Syracuse, New York, Goldman concluded that teachers in high rather than in low damage schools identified less with their school, they were less enthusiastic about teaching, they considered that parents were uninterested in or unfavourably disposed toward the school, and they were more concerned with impersonal factors like the administration, age or location of the building than with personal relations and their professional effectiveness. Pupils in high damage schools were relatively uninterested in academic work, did not identify with the school and had higher drop-out and truancy rates. Both teachers and pupils reported "...that the most significant factor in the causation of vandalism is an attitude of boredom in students. Such boredom might be evidence of indifference or a feeling that the curriculum is inappropriate to the needs of the student. Boredom may also result from a lack of rapport between students and teachers". These findings make good intuitive sense and fit well with the research completed in this country by Rutter et al (1979) into the importance of viewing schools as social institutions which could either foster or deter delinquency in their pupils.

A comprehensive review of the leading articles on school vandalism, carried out by Zwier and Vaughan in 1984, concluded that there were three ideological orientations - conservative, liberal and radical - running through most of the research and that it would be useful to be aware of these because **too often the choice of strategy to tackle vandalism "...depends less on its proven efficacy than on the values and attitudes of those concerned with the problem"** (p 263). Briefly, the conservative stance believes that vandalism is caused by sick, aberrant individuals who must be caught and punished; the school needs to be protected and the community organised into anti-vandal patrols. The liberal position, in contrast, highlights faults in the educational system rather than in individuals and admits a broader range of possible causes like an irrelevant curriculum, the quality of relationships between teacher and taught or the physical lay-out of the buildings. All of these are considered modifiable and an extension of leisure facilities for young people tends to be advocated. Finally, the radical approach finds the roots of school vandalism neither in the personality of individuals nor in malfunctions of the school system but in the structural problems created for young people by society. Community education and structural changes are therefore the favoured strategies of the radicals. We have met these differing explanations before (in Chapter 5 on motives and meanings) and only the terminology is different.

The main, practical implication of Zwier and Vaughan's classification system is that "...because the research exercise is inextricably bound up with the ideological orientation of the investigator, the role of the social scientist must change. Instead of trying to identify 'real' causes, the social scientist should..." (1984, p 285) use action research to monitor continually changes to specific situations, changes which he or she has co-operated in developing, introducing and assessing.

This is an honest attempt to rescue academic research on school vandalism from the morass into which it has fallen. After years of endeavour we are no closer to a consensus on either a definition or on the causes of vandalism, the field is riven with ideological disputes, and some of the findings which are reported are not worth the money they cost to produce eg "Children who dislike school commit vandalism much more often than children who enjoy going to school" (van Dijk et al, 1984, p 328). No wonder that recent years have seen a wholescale retreat from attempts to analyse the underlying reasons for vandalism and a corresponding explosion of interest in technological solutions. A typical publication now is one which deals dismissively with the complex issues of definition, motives and cost in an introduction of one page and then devotes the next eighty-four pages to the relative merits of "ultrasonic" or "microwave volumetric detectors" of intruders. The preferred strategy now is the technical fix which, in terms of Zwier and Vaughan's (1984) matrix, is a decidedly conservative orientation.

One example of this approach will serve as a useful introduction to the theme of the next chapter on prevention. The North East Regional Schools Security Group (NERSSG) was formed in 1985 to establish a co-ordinated, managed approach to the prevention of crime against the region's schools. So far, so good. In 1990 the Group produced a management guide to *Security in Schools,* whose one page introduction produces the statistics to legitimate increased expenditure on physical deterrents. It is claimed, for instance, that one school in fifteen in the UK "...can now be expected, statistically, to experience a fire during the course of the year" and that "A recent survey among local education authorities showed that they each expected an average of four crimes per day to be directed against schools in their area" (NERSSG, 1990, p 9).

The trouble with these and other statements are that they are based on the answers to a questionnaire sent to all 126 LEAs in England, Wales and Scotland; unfortunately, only 19 (or 15%) replied and, even among those who did, some did not know the number of incidents either of criminal damage or of fires in their schools or the costs involved. A frequent comment alongside the figures which were quoted by the 19 LEAs who replied was either "approximate" or "estimated". So the claims mentioned above have been extrapolated from a very small and rather unrepresentative sample in order to present a national picture for England and Wales; this practice must be treated with great caution. It is an improvement on guesswork but not much of one.

I remain in sympathy, however, with the authors of the NERSSG's report because my own attempts to prize comparable statistics out of LEAs in the North of England and in London similarly came to very little. LEAs, of course, receive numerous requests for information and were themselves involved at the time of my enquiry in a political struggle with central government over funding in their future role. The abolition of ILEA on 1st

April 1990 also allowed the 12 inner London Boroughs and the City of London, which became responsible for education in inner London, to claim that they had no historical records and were too newly formed to have reliable statistical information of their own. I received a number of invitations to speak to named officers with responsibility for these areas but it soon became clear that the information which I wanted was either not collected or was stored in such a form as to prevent useful comparisons with other educational authorities. It can only be hoped that the Department of Education and Science's national survey to gather solid, reliable data from a sample of 800 primary and 500 secondary schools proves more successful.

There is a further issue which practising teachers would like to see given more prominence in the debate on school vandalism: **the impact of dirty, poorly maintained and dilapidated buildings on the behaviour of young people**. The annual report of the Senior Chief Inspector of Schools (HMI, 1991, p 11) claims that, nationally, "...the general condition of the fabric of buildings and the state of internal decoration in many schools continue to be unsatisfactory". Locally, in the North East of England, I know of schools which have not been painted for twenty years or more, where the staff are ashamed of the toilets pupils have to use, and where the general atmosphere of physical neglect is inimical to learning. It is in such schools that graffiti and then vandalism take hold.

Teachers are not alone in seeing the connection between neglected buildings and poor behaviour. When anti-vandalism projects (such as the initiative in nearly 60 schools in the Strathclyde region) listen to the views and constructive suggestions of pupils, what is immediately apparent is the quality of their thinking, their commitment to change and their realism. Pupils at St Gregory's Secondary School in Glasgow, for example, argued that "if they are to have pride in the school, they want to feel that others are prepared to invest in maintaining the basic school structure..." and that "...the general drabness of the school interior makes it a depressing environment in which to learn" (Crime Concern Scotland, 1991a, p 9). Many pupils at Possilpark Secondary School, again in Glasgow, "...are concerned about the poor image of the school to outsiders and the effect this might have on their employment prospects..." and they "...do want to see change, especially if other agencies contribute to an all-round improvement in the school" (Crime Concern Scotland, 1991b, p 9).

When asked if they would be willing to participate in a 'stop vandalism within the school' campaign, pupils began proposing slogans, badges and logos within the small group discussions. And when it came to proposing suggestions, they supported, for instance, the idea of an authorised graffiti wall (an idea resisted by the teachers), being made responsible for their own common rooms, and opening the school out of hours for swimming, discos, sports and general community use. The pupils at Possilpark School also made the telling point that **too often in modern society there is simply no place for adolescents**: for example, swimming pools cater well for groups like mums and toddlers and organised school parties but rarely recognise the recreational needs of young people at weekends and during school holidays. If anything, this is the group that leisure centres seek to exclude. Pupils also commented upon "the lack of personal respect they felt from one or two teachers" which led them to have little respect for the school.

Enough has been said, I hope, to support the argument that in responding to vandalism and graffiti by means of crime prevention panels, **the most important resource in local communities may very well be the knowledge, enthusiasm and realism of young people**. Their involvement, in my view, is a necessary but not a sufficient condition for success: too many schools are currently set in a sea of unemployment and poverty which they and their pupils are impotent to change.

CHAPTER 9

PREVENTION

One of the surprises in producing this report has been that so much more has been written on strategies for prevention than on any other aspect of vandalism or graffiti. As mentioned in the first chapter, I collected almost five times as much material on solutions than on explanations. And yet, as we have already seen, the theoretical literature is in some considerable disarray. It therefore seems unlikely that preventative measures will be well developed, apposite and effective, if our understanding of the basic problems remains incomplete, confused and contested; and unfortunately a careful assessment of attempts at intervention confirms the accuracy of this speculation. Tim Hope (1984, p 335) has reflected on what we have learned from putting ideas about how to prevent vandalism into practice and his conclusion is far from encouraging: "In comparison with the range of theories about the causes of vandalism, our knowledge of how to prevent vandalism is severely limited".

The paradox is that, despite this "excess of theory over practical knowledge and experience" (Hope, ibid), writers have not felt constrained when elaborating their suggestions and, in the main, **the history of preventive measures has been innovation without evaluation**. Often the notion that intervention may actually cause more harm than good has not even been considered. Gladstone (1978, p 37), for instance, rightly cautioned that improving leisure opportunities for young people may lead to an increase rather than a decrease in vandalism by drawing "...boys onto the streets and into the company of a 'tough group' who would otherwise remain at home, quietly watching television". In other words, vandalism is one of those problems where **some of the preferred solutions may create more difficulties than the original offence**. Stan Cohen (1984b, p 232) sums up this point neatly: "Vandalism can easily become the sort of social problem where the cost and unintended consequences of the intervention simply create more problems: a case of social policy becoming what Spieber calls a 'fatal remedy'."

One way of conveying an impression of the muddle which the literature on prevention is in would be to set out the various classifying schemes which have so far been suggested in order to show the wide range of ideas which currently compete for attention. The experts have produced anything from one to nine main categories of measures to prevent vandalism and examples of some of the better known schemes are given below:

1. Oscar Newman (1972, p 204) is alone in settling for a single strategy, "...the only effective measure for assuring a safe living environment is community control" and he cannot resist having a side swipe at alternative measures, "short-term measures involving flights to suburbia or additional police manpower and equipment are only palliatives".

2. Van Vliet (1984, p 21) distinguishes between two general strategies directed at either the <u>physical</u> or at the <u>social</u> environment. The former emphasises short-term solutions, detailed checklists and guidelines for planners and architects, while the latter concentrates on long-term, individual or socio-structural factors. No further detail is given.

3. Five authors plump for three categories, which turns out to be the favourite number, and there is a measure of overlap between their suggestions. Gladstone (1980, p 139) lists three approaches to prevention: reducing the opportunities for offending; "social prevention which tries to counteract criminal motivation"; and reinforcing legal prohibitions. Wilson (1990, p 151) talks of three methods of intervention: awareness campaigns (Neighbourhood Watch, media publicity, etc); improved detection of offenders (eg offering rewards); and target hardening (eg plastic phone cards rather than coin boxes). Mawby (1977, p 31) also discusses three solutions: greater law enforcement by increasing the reporting of offences; increasing penalties on those caught; and making property "vandal-proof". Stan Cohen (1984a, p 59) names three strategies: physical (design improvement); social (community involvement, education); and deterrent (surveillance, tenant patrols). There are three overlapping categories according to Baker and Waddon (1989, p 169): environmental (increasing security and ecological change like improved housing); systemic (community participation and institutional change); and behavioural (changing attitudes and increasing the accountability of parents).

4. The work of four researchers is considered here. Herbert (1990, p 67) refers to "four foci for preventative work in schools": the material environment (locks, patrols etc); the individual (productive activities including murals by pupils); the school system (encouraging a positive school ethos); and the local community (extend Neighbourhood Watch schemes to include School Watch). With specific reference to graffiti, May (1989, pp 8-10) describes an amnesty campaign and the offer of legitimate murals to young 'graffitists' in New York; imaginative programmes to

divert their energies elsewhere were also introduced and 'tags' were removed quickly to reduce the motivation to 'get up'. The practical guide *Crime Prevention in School* produced by the Department of Education and Science (1987, p 7) reviews four types of prevention: security measures; management approaches (good housekeeping practices); design changes to reduce the vulnerability of particular targets; and strategic planning (directing resources where they are most needed). A strategic approach to prevention has four key elements according to Henry Giller (1988, p 33): discrete, local community-based interventions; the need to incorporate all those, including local businesses, who live, work and service the community; evaluation of every initiative; and co-ordination of all programmes.

5. Only one entry. The NERSSG (1990, p 13) report sets out five principal avenues for consideration: consultation with experts; procedural improvements to reduce opportunities; physical and electronic protection; introducing crime prevention into the curriculum; and community involvement.

6. In an earlier paper (1973b), Stan Cohen detailed not three (as above) but six main approaches to prevention: defeatism (resignation, damage is written off as inevitable); deflection (the behaviour is channelled into what are considered to be more constructive alternatives); utilitarian prevention (devising techniques to protect property); education and publicity (make the public more aware of the seriousness and the cost of vandalism); deterrence and retribution (clamp down hard); and primary prevention (strike at the roots of the malaise: the home, the school and the permissive society). Islington Council has developed six "principles of intervention" (Jones, 1988, p 23): successful policing depends on public co-operation; most control of anti-social behaviour is achieved by the public; most offenders are unaware of the consequences of their actions, so they need to be educated about the fear and distress they cause; much crime is minor and poorly motivated and so can be avoided by target hardening; victim support is as important as crime control; and successful intervention is multi-agency.

7. For once, the magic number seven has no takers that I am aware of.

8. NACRO (1988, p 16) has based its play and youth policy on eight principles: encouraging a positive attitude towards children and young people by policy makers; a commitment to consulting and involving

children and young people; all residential areas require a <u>range</u> of facilities; some provision (eg youth clubs) is a collective rather than a parental responsibility; maintaining a balance between the input of the local authority and that of the local community; special initiatives for groups excluded from mainstream provision; and encouraging young people to have a positive attitude to their community.

9. Two entries. Zwier and Vaughan (1984, p 271) produce a list of nine strategies: writing-off, functional alternatives, technological, social/ structural (eg rules in school), educative, legal-primitive, therapeutic, co-operative and societal change. Clarke (1978, p 76) produced an overview of the implications for prevention of the Home Office Research Unit's studies on vandalism and highlighted the following: parents should instil greater respect for property in their children; publicity campaigns to do the same; parents should exercise greater supervision over their children; more leisure facilities for 'tough' youths; making school more attractive to 'tough' youths; families with young children to be dispersed in public housing estates; more police patrols; more punitive action by the courts; and more protection for vulnerable public property (at this point I will spare the reader a further list of eight suggestions).

Where have we got to? Reading and re-reading all these suggested approaches to prevention and control has brought home to me that some commentators are referring to different levels of intervention or contradictory conceptions of the problem; that others are simply using different terminology to refer to the same basic idea and are aware that their strategies are not mutually exclusive; and that others still are concentrating on different stages of the process of offending. Jones (1988, p 23), for instance, is one of the few authors to refer explicitly to the time dimension "...anti-crime education acts on the motivation to commit crime; target hardening reduces the possibility; public/police co-operation enhances the detection rate; and victim support alleviates the after effects of the crime". Having said that, the list of categories from one to nine given above contains more than fifty, separate preventative measures and that list is by no means exhaustive. Immediately, then, we can conclude that **there is no panacea and no consensus where prevention is concerned**.

What options are we left with? Choosing the preferred solutions of our favourite expert or an eclectic group of measures which intuitively seem to be worth trying? Deciding to back all the horses in the race and to implement simultaneously all 50+ measures in the list? Or concentrating on those whose effectiveness has been clearly demonstrated? On this latter point, the evidence is both patchy and contradictory; van Vliet (1984, pp 22-23), for example, studied fourteen intervention programmes, six of which provided no information on either implementation or evaluation, one reported an increase in vandalism and seven claimed reductions. But even in these successful cases, the assessments were not sufficiently comprehensive to allow extrapolations of what particular aspects of the intervention had been effective, in what combination and under which conditions. We have, in other words, no systematic body of evaluative knowledge which allows us to say, for instance, that the level of vandalism on this housing estate can be diminished by applying this approach (or combination of approaches) for six months at this level of intensity and cost, and covering these sections of the population. We are a long way from this level of sophisticated knowledge and control.

There are, in fact, a number of problems which either lessen or eliminate the effectiveness of the best thought out preventive programmes and Baker and Waddon (1989, p 170) have enumerated the main ones: high cost, instability over time (eg community self-help), authoritarian undertones, administrative difficulties, political unacceptability, minimal impact, difficult to implement, and lack of public participation. There is no need, however, to wring our hands in collective frustration and pessimism. There are some broad, historical trends in our response to crime and vandalism which can be discerned and there are also lessons which can be learned from the careful evaluation of attempts to implement a planned programme of prevention. These will now be described.

Henri Giller (1988, p 4) has identified **three radical changes in our understanding over the last twenty years**. The first of these is "...**the moving away from reliance upon the individual offender as the focus for crime prevention initiatives**". The traditional approach has been to track down the "tiny minority" of those responsible for "mindless" criminal damage, label them "vandals" and "treat" them by means of fines or periods of incarceration. But the demonstration by Gladstone (1978) that vandalism was widely prevalent among young boys and by Pollard (1988) that large numbers of young girls were also involved, coupled with the acknowledged failure of fines or residential treatment to change individual behaviour (see Rutter and Giller, 1983) all undermined credibility in the traditional responses to vandalism; except, that is, for the mass media which continue to carry stereotypes of the 'typical' vandal.

Second, **the last twenty years have also witnessed the growth of what has come to be called the 'situational' approach to prevention**, which, despite being over-sold in the early days of its introduction, has become a central instrument of policy and so deserves to have its strengths and weaknesses explained in detail. As official dismay mounted about the constantly rising levels of crime, the ineffectiveness, and the spiralling costs, of residential treatment (see Cornish and Clarke, 1975), attention turned to tackling crime by manipulating the environment in order to reduce the opportunities (both the material conditions and the risk) for crime. This represented a change from trying to alter the personalities or the deep-seated, anti-social attitudes of convicted offenders. This 'situational' approach covers a number of different types of measure, each of which will be briefly outlined.

Target hardening, for example, increases the physical security of property and one of the first successes of the technique was the introduction of locks to the steering wheels of cars which immediately reduced the level of car thefts by 60% (Mayhew et al, 1980a) but no longer prevents young 'joy-riders' from stealing cars. Other targets of crime are removed altogether (by, for instance, paying staff by cheque rather than by cash). The means of committing crime can also be removed by, say, prohibiting children by law from buying aerosol paint sprays. The incentives to crime can be reduced as well by, for example, marking video recorders and cameras with indelible codes. Formal surveillance (by the police, special patrols or private security firms), informal surveillance (by the general public) and surveillance by employees (caretakers in schools and on housing estates) can all help to deter potential offenders. Finally, the social environment can be manipulated to reduce opportunities for crime in ways suggested by environmental psychologists like Levy-Leboyer who, as explained in Chapter 1, favour a socio-environmental approach to vandalism. Marcus (1984, p 318) records how British Telecom have adopted a new stance which views "...the payphone and its vandalism as part of the community in which it is sited" and have been experimenting with their kiosks being "fostered" as part of the community; they have also encouraged "vandal and pre-vandal age children" to adopt a phone-box.

Some disadvantages with the 'situational' approach soon became apparent, however; it has little to say about reducing the levels of violent street crime and is mainly concerned with property offences. In addition, target hardening was interpreted by some young people as a challenge and Sloan-Howitt and Kelling (1990) reported how target hardening failed when 'graffitists' learned to cut through the wire fences which were erected to protect the subway trains. Similarly, the development of more and more sophisticated techniques for removing and controlling graffiti (see Wallace and Whitehead, 1989) has involved "the other side" in an ever escalating "arms race" to find paints which cannot be removed even by the most advanced detergents.

Displacement of offences to an adjacent area is another unintended consequence of the 'situational approach' to crime reduction. Equipping certain London Underground stations with closed circuit television apparently displaced some incidents of theft to nearby stations (Burrows, 1980). The enthusiasts for the approach (Hough et al, 1980, p 17) would have us believe that "...the extent of displacement has been considerably overestimated", but evidence continues to mount (Newman, 1972; May, 1989; Wilson, 1990) that it does take place. The DES Bulletin (1987, p 3) on crime prevention in schools is careful to point out that evaluation of preventive measures needs to "...include all schools within the administrative area of the authority so that an estimate of any displacement effects may be attempted" (emphasis as in original).

A third type of difficulty concerns the wholesale retreat of some authorities into locks, alarms, floodlights and electronic security systems. Few, if any, would dispute that, when school arsonists are inflicting damage estimated at a hundred million a year in Britain, all schools need to become more security conscious and to develop a policy to minimise risks. On the other hand, TVS/British Telecom's (1990) video programme on vandalism describes a primary school in Knowsley, Merseyside which, after being destroyed by three fires in less than two years, was rebuilt along the following lines. It "...is surrounded by a nine foot steel stockade. A few small ground-floor windows made from unbreakable plastic are encased in shutters immediately lessons are over; the doors are made of steel; floodlights illuminate the playground at night and infra-red intruder alarms monitor any movement in classrooms and corridors".

Socrates was one of the first to argue that the bodies and minds of the young are affected by their surroundings and that the future guardians of society should dwell in a wholesome climate where "...some influence from noble works constantly falls upon eye and ear from childhood upward, and imperceptibly draws them into sympathy and harmony with the beauty of reason..." (Plato, *The Republic*, III, 401).

Some of our children attend schools and universities whose buildings nourish the soul as well as the mind; but others learn different lessons in primary schools which are turned into fortresses and sealed off each evening from their local community. What price equality of opportunity or parity of esteem in Knowsley? That is not to say that we as a society should meekly pick up the enormous bill for school fires, but rather that there needs to be some middle course between, on the one hand, constructing schools for 5 to 11 year-olds which resemble prisons for adults and, on the other, leaving our schools dangerously unprotected. There is now a wealth of sound, practical advice available to schools (those interested should consult DES, 1983, 1987, 1988 and 1989) both on the design and maintenance of buildings and on strategies for prevention. Specifically on the issue of costs, the NERSSG (1990, p 55) suggests that (based on 1989 prices in the North East) a primary school could install an adequate security system for between £2,000 and £2,500 and a comprehensive school for between £6,000 and £7,000. Extreme defensive measures are likely to prove disproportionate, unduly expensive and counter-productive in that they may hinder a school from developing relationships with its local community. In practical terms and in spite of all the extravagant claims of the manufacturers, these security systems too often prove to be inefficient; alarms are activated by high winds or heavy traffic so frequently that the police eventually stop responding. Similarly, technical difficulties still bedevil the electronic monitoring of offenders (see Mair and Nee, 1990), which is no longer regarded as the panacea to prison overcrowding.

The third theme in our changing response to rising levels of crime and vandalism is well captured by Henri Giller (1988, p 5) himself. **How are we, he asks, "...to generate community cohesion** so as to reconstitute the confidence of local people in their ability to regulate their own environment and the behaviour of people within it?" To help answer his question, the example of Neighbourhood Watch will be studied as an index of the growing public concern about crime prevention. Steve Norris (1988, p 32) has recorded how Neighbourhood Watch began in 1982 with one scheme in this country and developed within six years into 50,000 schemes involving more than a quarter of a million volunteers and more than 400 crime prevention panels up and down the country. By April 1991 there were 92,000 schemes in England and Wales, covering around 5 million households, according to a speech by the Home Secretary, Kenneth Baker (1991, p 4). The basic principle behind all such movements is the attempt to rebuild within our communities the informal processes of social control which have been so eroded that many citizens (and not just the old) have been rendered fearful and isolated because of crime. Jane Jacobs (1961, pp 31-32), in a justly famous passage, eloquently stated the basic principle thus: **"The first thing to understand is that the public peace...is not kept primarily by the police, necessary as police are. It is kept primarily by an intricate unconscious network of voluntary controls and standards among the people themselves, and enforced by the people themselves."**

So collective action by groups of residents or neighbours in order to control crime, to reduce the fear of crime, to recreate community cohesion and to restore confidence in the police and the criminal justice system is a further,

Does Neighbourhood Watch actually increase rather than decrease the fear of crime?

officially sanctioned step away from the traditional response to crime which focussed on individual criminals. A key Home Office objective is to "develop and strengthen community institutions" (quoted by Norris, 1988, p 32) in the fight against crime and, according to Kenneth Baker (1991, p 3), Neighbourhood Watch, together with its derivatives Farm Watch, Vehicle Watch and Business Watch, is "...a key element in cracking crime". But is the strategy effective? **What hard evidence is there that Neighbourhood Watch has made an appreciable difference to crime figures?** Is it possible that such meetings actually <u>heighten</u> the fear of crime as neighbours exchange information about local incidents which may not have been widely known?

Dennis Rosenbaum (1987, p 127), in a critical overview of the theory and research behind Neighbourhood Watch in the United States, found a paucity of rigorous experimental evaluations. What evidence did exist led him to conclude that "...if given the opportunity to participate, residents in the majority of high-crime neighbourhoods would not participate and when citizens do participate, the social interaction that occurs at meetings may lead to increases (rather than decreases) in fear of crime...". In other words, it was largely middle-class people from stable residential areas who were joining such organisations, whereas "...neighbourhoods that need the most help (ie have the most serious crime problems) will be the least receptive to such programs because these residential areas are characterised by suspicion, distrust, hostility and a lack of shared norms regarding appropriate public behaviour" (1987, p 115). The implications of his work are <u>not</u> that we abandon the objective of involving more citizens in crime prevention but rather that our intervention programmes need to be solidly grounded and critically assessed for effectiveness. In this country, the *British Crime Survey* (Mayhew et al, 1989) has assessed the impact of Neighbourhood Watch and replicated most of Rosenbaum's findings in that members tended to be better-off, owner-occupiers from affluent suburban areas, and that there was no definitive proof that the scheme reduced crime or the fear of crime.

It seems appropriate, then, to end this chapter by examining the experience of an action research project which involved a number of agencies (police, local officials and the staff of schools) in a co-ordinated programme to combat vandalism in the schools of an inner-city area in the North of England (see Gladstone, 1978, 1980 and Hope, 1984). The project was intended to test the 'situational' approach to the prevention of vandalism and to draw upon all relevant local resources in a demonstration "...which might serve as a model for others to emulate" (Hope, 1984, p 335). Many of the successes of the project have already been incorporated into this report as can be judged from the number of quotations from, and references to, the work of Gladstone and Hope. But, despite having an unprecedented level of detailed information on, and a sophisticated analysis of, vandalism at individual schools, and having developed a multiple strategy to tackle it, the project "...failed to alter, in any appreciable way, the response by the local authorities" (Hope, 1984, p 340).

There is often more to be gained from studying the mistakes of others than from trying to draw lessons from 'good practice' which is often so successful as to be intimidating. First, when the decision-makers were presented with a variety of recommendations based on the situational analysis provided by Gladstone (1978), they invariably chose physical measures (eg target hardening) rather than social initiatives (eg increased leisure provision). This led Hope (1984, p 339) to reflect that the irony of collaborative decision-making is that "...decisions which command the greatest support may often be those which are least innovative because they are least controversial". Corroboration of this conclusion comes from an architect's attempt (Wawrzynski, 1984, p 293) to combine social and design elements in a preventive scheme in Oldham. But only physical modifications were introduced and that without consulting the tenants, while radical changes in management were largely ignored. He pointed to the need for <u>preventive</u> measures (caretakers, changes in the housing allocation policy, etc) to be introduced as well as <u>defensive</u> measures.

Second, although the project ran into difficulties at each of its three phases - planning, decision-making and implementation - most of the main obstacles were encountered when trying to <u>implement</u> the preventive measures. Three specific difficulties were identified and one more general problem. For all the confident sales talk of the security experts, unanticipated technical difficulties prevented, for instance, the installation of any toughened glass. Moreover, local misunderstandings and inadequate supervision resulted in environmental changes being only partially introduced; and an "imperfect" system of recording vandalism (to monitor the effectiveness of the innovations) was replaced by an "inadequate" one. Besides, co-ordination between different agencies failed to materialise.

Norman Tutt (1988, p 26) has drawn on his experience of academia and of running Social Work Departments to explain why inter-agency co-operation happens so rarely; he has pointed to the very different perspectives and priorities which professionals from a variety of disciplines bring to bear on a problem, the differential power and managerial style of, say, a Chief Superintendent of Police and an Assistant Education Officer, and the need for agreed objectives and processes right from the beginning.

With the unfair advantage of hindsight, I would describe the general problem with the 'situational' approach as a pervading political naiveté, coupled with the absence of a model of change, which would have predicted successive waves of difficulty (see Nisbet, 1975) and which would also have refused to call inevitable difficulties "failure" (Constable, 1986). But perhaps the researchers themselves should be given the last word:

> *Although the situational approach is valuable in directing attention to local circumstances, its scope needs to be broadened to include the organisational and political arena in which prevention is to be initiated. Above all, there is a continuing need to find a better fit between theory and practical experience. Situational approaches to vandalism prevention may have narrowed the gap between theory and practice, but the experience of this demonstration project, at least, suggests there is still a long way to go (Hope, 1984, p 342).*

CHAPTER 10

RECOMMENDATIONS

Keeping one's critical faculties well honed is a necessary precondition for reading accounts of interviews and preventive action, especially when charismatic enthusiasts are convinced of the effectiveness of their ideas even before they have been implemented. But the reward for such vigilance is the taste of dust in one's mouth as programme after programme proves to be either unassessed, or ineffective, or a mixed blessing, where it is difficult to disentangle what has been successful from what has not, because a combination of strategies has been used simultaneously. The end result is that one becomes hungry for good, or at least encouraging, news. Some such appears to be emerging from Paris, Lyons and Marseilles as a result of the French response to the riots in the ghettoes during "L'été chaud" of 1981, the year of similar riots in Brixton and Toxteth.

Michael King (1988) describes how the French responded with a radical programme of action which went far beyond the recommendations of Lord Scarman's (1981) enquiry into the Brixton disorders. For example, they set up a network of *Missions Locales* in all the major cities and most of the large towns throughout the country. The central goals of this initiative reflect **a typically continental approach to the structural position of young adults in society, stressing as it does social integration, community action, and giving young adults responsibility, training and employment rather than recruiting more police officers as has happened in Britain** with a 15% increase in manpower in the last ten years. King (1988, p 23) describes *Missions Locales* as places "...for young people between the ages of 16 and 25 to discuss problems of job training, employment, accommodation and finance with people with the knowledge and expertise to propose solutions and help to put them into effect". The *Missions Locales* are the most permanent, structural feature of the French policy of crime prevention but they are only established in localities where the social, economic, administrative and political forces first demonstrate their willingness to work together. To quote King (1988, p 34) again "...the objectives of many of the projects are long-term ones, aimed at social integration and job acquisition, as well as building confidence and a positive self-image rather than at an immediate cut in crime". Reductions of around 10% in the types of crime typically committed by young people (eg vandalism and theft) have since been claimed by the French authorities but whether these can be directly attributed to the community approach to crime prevention must await more systematic evaluation than has so far been completed.

French programmes of crime prevention have not been introduced here as a panacea or even as a blue print for Britain to copy. The riots in the Sartrouville suburb of Paris over Easter 1991 between police and youths of North African origin suggest that much has still to be done to integrate immigrant communities. Rather, the French response to urban riots serves to introduce an important point, namely, that **a narrow concentration on reducing vandalism and graffiti may prove to be self-defeating**; instead, opportunities have been provided for young adults to rejoin educational courses, to start occupational training, to find jobs or accommodation, to discuss difficulties with literacy, money, drugs or parents, and to become involved in organising and running leisure activities and holiday camps. Any reduction in criminal statistics is seen as a by-product of policies which are considered to be worth pursuing in their own right. That is a cultural difference between ourselves and the French (and other continental countries) which we may be reluctant to adopt because "...we prefer the social problems which surround us to the consequences of deliberate and heroic efforts to change the culture" (Ward, 1990, p 9, drawing on the work of Paul Tappan).

It is an argument which Stan Cohen (1984a, p 60) has consistently made to English speaking audiences:

> ...whether or not the construction of a needed playground for children on a public housing estate actually reduces rates of vandalism should never determine whether or not to support such programmes. Such reforms are to be justified for their own sake or not at all. We are in favour of adequate play facilities, decent housing, creative education or whatever because we are in favour of them - not because they are alleged to reduce vandalism.

For readers who have ploughed through nine chapters of my reservations, criticisms and unconscious biases, there ought to be a reward which spells out what lessons can be learned from previous efforts to prevent vandalism in Britain and elsewhere. What follows is obviously a personal selection in no particular order of priority, which attempts to home in on the key issues rather than to provide a list of sources of practical help which can be found in the Appendix. This chapter will then end with a few personal observations in an attempt to avoid the trap, mentioned in the previous chapter, of accepting only those suggestions which would be acceptable to the majority of commentators.

Whatever measures are proposed, they will also need to meet the three criteria of legitimacy, feasibility and support which Hall et al (1975) have identified as the reasons why certain issues rather than others become the source of new social policy. If these three criteria are applied to the present case, then proposals to deal with vandalism would, I suggest, be widely considered to be a <u>legitimate</u> concern of government; they would need to undergo tests of <u>feasibility</u> (eg the cost of the proposals, do they call for new patterns of collaboration among organisations and are they administratively feasible); and how widespread would be the <u>support</u> (eg whose discontents and whose satisfactions are involved) enjoyed by the new policies. If, however, vandalism were to be linked to the rising crime figures which, according to Rose (1991, p 24) have "...reached record levels, accompanied by social and political panic", then it is more likely to be treated as a priority issue. On the other hand, those who suffer most from crime and criminal damage tend to be the most powerless sections of the community and so less likely to translate their discontent into political pressure.

1. A MULTIPLE APPROACH AND A MODEL OF CHANGE

Does anyone really expect a single initiative such as Neighbourhood Watch to reverse on its own the seemingly inexorable rise in the levels of crime generally and of vandalism in particular? Any problem which is as varied, deep-seated and resistant to change as vandalism will need **a multiple, co-ordinated strategy, operating simultaneously at various levels**. Experience, which we have already drawn on (Tutt, 1984; Hope, 1984) in the previous chapter on prevention, has made clear the most common obstacles to successful inter-agency co-operation and the main difficulties encountered during the stage of implementation. A common theme to emerge is the need to tackle "...the bureaucratic web which controls most cities" (Canter, 1984, p 355) in a way which makes both innovation and evaluation acceptable. No easy task.

Indeed, any reasonably objective assessment of the major attempts at social reform in this country or in the United States in the last thirty years would conclude that, with few exceptions, they have failed and failed spectacularly. What lies at the heart of such failures? Fullan's (1982, p 4) answer is "Neglect of the phenomenology of change - that is, how people actually experience change as distinct from how it might have been intended". His sophisticated, elaborate and appealing thesis can only be referred to in passing here. Essentially, what he is arguing is that, in addition to an explicit programme of changes which we want to introduce, **we also need an explicit *model* of change** which pays due attention to the subjective realities of all those involved in implementing the changes. And one of the obstacles to successful change (space precludes the discussion of more than one) is the failure to recognise that managing change is, what he calls, a "multivariate" business, namely, the ability to deal with a large number of complex factors at different levels at the same time. In his own words:

> *We must remember that there are a set of interacting factors which impinge on attempts at change, even though we find it psychologically more reassuring to deal with one factor at a time. What is required is <u>multivariate</u> thinking - attention to <u>all</u> the factors that interact with each other in the change process (Fullan, 1982, p 29, emphasis as in original).*

2. HOUSING POLICY

Anne Power (1989, p 232) has characterised recent developments in housing policy as a retreat from bigger and bigger units to the decentralisation of management to estates which are smaller; where tenants are consulted about physical design, allocation procedures and facilities; and where resident caretakers deter vandalism. This latter point is one of the generally agreed findings in the literature at least since the publication of the Lambeth Inner Area Study in 1977 (Department of the Environment), but instead of being acted upon, the supervision of many large estates has been reduced to one or no resident caretaker. "The caretakers themselves, increasingly isolated and often nakedly exposed to tenant dissatisfaction, demanded protection or withdrawal" (Power, 1989, p 213).

This raises the issue of **the supervision of public facilities** generally, not just housing estates but also railway stations and buses, where Sturman (1980, p 38) found in Manchester that the absence of conductors "...was the most important factor affecting the amount of damage sustained". It is difficult to resist Colin Ward's (1990, p 2) conclusion that we have reached the stage in Britain where "...it is easier to suffer the endless diminution of public facilities than to ensure that they are protected".

When the residents of vandalised estates have been consulted, as they were by the GLC in 1984, they tend to claim that the key to prevention lies in the involvement of the tenants in all aspects of life on their estates to counteract the remoteness and ineffectiveness of management. Again, Colin Ward (1990, p 6) has been right to remind us that it was Oscar Newman who put tenant participation and local control back on the political agenda. More recently, research studies (eg Cairncross et al, 1989) have examined the mechanisms used to develop tenant participation in housing management in order to suggest good practice in terms of targets and standards to Local Authorities, Housing Associations and private landlords.

The reasons which are commonly advanced to support tenant participation are that it will encourage community development, improve housing management, give the tenants more choice and power, increase their satisfaction and improve the relationships with councillors and housing committee members. But do all the tenants in ghetto estates, struggling as they are against an intricate web of interlocking deprivations such as unemployment, poverty and lack of training facilities, want to participate? Markus (1988, p 11) provides the following answer to that question:

> It may not even be the area over which people necessarily want control; given reasonable initial standards and good maintenance and repair, they may wish to be relieved of this burden so as to be free to concentrate their energies on other aspects of their lives where so much needs to be done.

3. EDUCATION, TRAINING AND EMPLOYMENT

What I want for my own two children is a first-class general education, an appropriate vocational qualification and a job worthy of a human being. In the last twenty years too many of us have stood on the sidelines and watched the introduction of sub-standard, government schemes (YOP, YTS, YT, CPVE, ET, etc) which have been developed for other people's children. If Stan Cohen's explanation (1973a, p 53) of the most prevalent form of vandalism (as a solution to the problems created by society for particular sections of working-class young people) is valid, then "...it follows also that this 'solution' will increase in frequency and intensity. For as the contradictions of our educational system become more apparent, the demands for occupational qualifications upgraded, the pool of unemployed juveniles widened and viable political solutions seem more remote, so will the potential for such delinquency increase".

Almost twenty years later, the Senior Chief Inspector of Schools in his annual report (HMI, 1991, para 9) is writing of worryingly poor standards among particular groups of pupils:

> *They include the children caught up in that stubborn statistic of around 30%*
> *poorly provided for in the compulsory years of primary and secondary schooling:*
> *the less academically able who continue to suffer disproportionately from*
> *whatever chronic or acute problems affect the education service; those primary*
> *pupils learning to read in one of the 20% of schools in which the teaching of*
> *reading is poor, and pupils in some inner-city schools where teacher turnover is*
> *such that continuity in learning and high standards of achievement are virtually*
> *impossible.*

Instead of an imaginative, over-arching and comprehensive plan for the education, training and employment of 16-25 year-olds in the United Kingdom, we have a whole raft of policies emanating from different Departments of State which are fragmented, incremental and contradictory. I have discussed these issues at length elsewhere (eg Coffield, 1991a), but there is space here for only two examples to make the case. In 1988 the Secretary of State for Education and Science markedly increased his centralising powers by introducing a national curriculum for 5-16 year-olds (notice not for 5-19 year-olds); within six months the Department of Employment was decentralising the system of training through the new Training and Enterprise Councils. Second, before the passing of the Education Reform Act (1988), schools tended to be cushioned against criminal damage or loss of stolen property which were both made good by the local authority. Now under Local Management of Schools, each institution, irrespective of the catchment it serves, will have to pay the cost of vandalism or theft from its own limited budget. So money spent on replacing windows or removing graffiti will not be available for science equipment or swimming. The policy is likely to exacerbate differences between schools serving run-down, inner-city areas and those situated in leafy suburbs.

A new Act of Parliament needs to be introduced to deal specifically with the education, training and employment of 16-19 year-olds (see Coffield, 1991b for details). Briefly, the options for all young adults need to be enhanced and providing them with equal benefits (means tested like student grants), may help to create more equal status among young people, whether they stay on at school or further education, enter an improved Youth Training Scheme leading to nationally recognised qualifications or high level apprenticeships targeted at skill shortages. Such educational reforms need to be matched by employment legislation to ensure that all employees are statutorily entitled to further education and training. And even if all these measures are passed into law, there will still need to be sufficient jobs to make use of the education, training and skills which have been acquired.

A number of commentators (eg Jones, 1988; NERSSG, 1990) have suggested that anti-vandalism education should be included in the national curriculum for all 5-16 year-olds, perhaps as part of one of the cross-curricular themes concerned with citizenship. No doubt pupils would benefit from such exposure and I have a specific suggestion to make later, but my reading of the literature on vandalism suggests that another group in society is more in need of such education, namely, the moral entrepreneurs of society: the senior police officers, the local councillors and the national politicians who speak regularly at conferences on vandalism but who apparently learn little, if anything, from them.

4. A NATIONAL POLICY FOR YOUTH

When Dennis Pollard (1988, p 55) invited his sample of 13-16 year-olds to make any comments they wanted after completing his questionnaire, one 15 year-old girl explained her involvement in vandalism in this manner: "We have no other way to put our points of view over, and walls, fences etc are the only way we can communicate with people in authority (we can't vote)". Another wrote simply "Let kids have a share in the appearance of the town" (Ibid).

It is now over twenty years since I first became professionally interested in social issues like juvenile delinquency and, during that period, **the plea to involve young people in the democratic process** has become a predictable recommendation which tends to make its ineffectual appearance in the final chapter of reports like this. Year after year, adults with power and influence wring their hands in anguish over the rising tide of 'teenage lawlessness' and either vote for more punitive law and order measures or restrict the participation of young people to a manipulative tokenism. For, as G K Chesterton memorably remarked about Christianity, **participation has not**

been tried and found wanting, it has been found difficult and left untried.

Sherry Arnstein (1969, p 216), reflecting on her experience of some of the largest federal programmes against poverty and slum housing in the States during the 1960s, has delineated eight levels of participation from manipulation and therapy (really, forms of non-participation), at the bottom of the ladder, to partnership and citizen control at the top; but the fundamental point is that "...participation without redistribution of power is an empty and frustrating process for the powerless".

This is not the place to specify a fully-developed youth policy but some of the essential features, which have been outlined by Bernard Davies (1986), would be to raise the expectations young adults have of themselves, to increase their ability to compete for jobs, to strengthen their capacity for collective action, and to work with them as partners. With specific relevance to vandalism and graffiti, the aim would be for local communities to recognise that **the people who are most informed about such behaviour and its meaning for those involved are young adults whose ideas and energy therefore need to be built into any preventive programme**. Young people are also quick to spot that much vandalism is self-defeating; they are unable to ring their friends or summon help, if the local call-box has been deliberately put out of action.

Recently, the Gulbenkian Foundation have funded a growing number of organisations - the London Union of Youth Clubs whose work on graffiti art was discussed in Chapter 6; the Council for Posterity which invites school classes to adopt a little piece of the planet, which is then improved by pupils acting as 'Planetary Guardians'; Crime Concern which makes grants of up to £200 to young people who start anti-vandalism projects like adopting and protecting damaged telephone kiosks or street lights, and which has started a pilot project in the Sandwell area on the effects of alcohol abuse on vandalism and other crime; the Safe Neighbourhoods Unit which helps clients "to devise innovative and cost-effective solutions" to problems associated with housing and crime and is specifically evaluating educational materials for primary school children on the topics of crime prevention and anti-vandalism; and Priority Area Development which is evaluating the effectiveness of Pupil Councils in Toxteth (Merseyside) schools in countering vandalism and bullying. Other areas like the Penrhys Community in the Rhondda Valley are producing a report on the best ways

Vandalism can become self-defeating. How do you ring friends or summon help if the local call-box has been deliberately put out of action?

of preventing vandalism. What all these projects have in common is **the willingness to listen to young people, to draw upon their knowledge, enthusiasm and commitment and to treat them as equals**; they are also being consulted about the causes of vandalism and preventive measures. Tapping the creativity of young adults is a sensible strategy in any anti-vandalism campaign but it needs to be emphasised that a <u>national</u> youth policy is being recommended because of its intrinsic value and not because it may lead to a reduction in vandalism; after all, not all criminal damage is committed by young people, a point to which I shall return shortly.

PERSONAL OBSERVATIONS

First, whatever elements are brought together in whatever strength and combination to form an anti-vandalism strategy, **the resourcing of the response needs to be proportionate to the size of the problem**. The clamour created by politicians about social problems tends to be in inverse proportions to the amount of money they allocate to their amelioration; and vandalism is no exception to the general rule. The DES, for instance, in 1990/91 has allocated an Education Support Grant of £2 million for the reduction of vandalism and arson in schools which is alleged to cost more than £100 million a year (Dean and Reid, 1990). The money will be used to install protective systems in 435 schools out of a national total of around 25,000 (DES, 1990, p 5).

There also needs to be a self-denying ordinance on the part of Ministers not to waste whatever sums they make available on expensive but ineffective media campaigns, which are close to the heart of ambitious, publicity-conscious politicians. Riley (1980), for example, evaluated three television campaigns in north west England whose objectives were to deter young people from vandalism by stressing the risk of being caught and to make parents more aware of their responsibilities in supervising their own children. The study concluded that no reliable evidence could be found of any significant effects of the advertising on television on either parents' attitudes or the level of offences. The reasons advanced by Riley (1980, p 137) for the failure deserve to be quoted in full:

...firstly, that potential offenders are unlikely to be moved by exhortation or generalised threats unless they have reason to believe that the actual risks and consequences of detection are worsened; and, secondly, that remote advertising

*messages may stand little chance of competing with the immediate pressures
operating at the time an offence is being considered.*

The research community has amassed over recent years abundant evidence
about the ineffectiveness of media campaigns to change people's attitudes
and, especially, behaviour. There is, for instance, a valid and reliable body of
knowledge detailing such failures in the field of health education (see, for
instance, Naidoo, 1986); but Ministers of both main parties continue to
throw good money after bad because political considerations (national
publicity) heavily outweigh the findings from research (about
ineffectiveness).

Specifically, we need something more effective than ephemeral and highly
expensive television adverts to convince adults of all ages about the health
risks involved in regularly drinking to excess. In 1986, health education
campaigns, aimed at encouraging sensible drinking, cost £3 million; in the
same year the brewers spent £200 million on advertising and promotion and
the government received £6,000 million in tax revenues from alcohol. The
social costs (especially to the Health Service) of alcohol misuse in Britain
have been estimated at anything between £2-10 billion.

Far and away the foremost health risks to young people in this country stem
<u>not</u> from heroin nor from cocaine nor AIDS, but from alcohol; and
government policy should reflect that finding. A strategic switch needs to be
made from mass media campaigns to providing information, and
attempting to change attitudes and behaviour through education. Small
group discussions in school for all twelve year-olds should be run by
sensitive teachers who are trusted by the pupils. Alcohol education should
be the main focus of such meetings but other health education issues such
as smoking, illegal drugs, sex education, crime prevention and vandalism
could also be tackled in such groups. Sufficient <u>resource</u> needs to be found to
prepare teachers, health co-ordinators and youth and community workers
for such work and sufficient <u>time</u> needs to be found within the National
Curriculum; at present the concentration on the main subjects (English,
Maths, Science, etc) is in danger of squeezing personal and social education
out of the timetable.

We could also introduce fiscal incentives to encourage safer drinking. The
Scandinavian countries have experimented successfully with clearly
labelling beers 1, 2 and 3 as they increase in strength, taxes have been

significantly reduced on the lower alcohol drinks, and so a market for super light beers and wines has been created. Tuck (1989, p 68) has also suggested staggering pub closing times to reduce the concentration of young drinkers all pouring out on to the streets at the same time. The brewing industry and the police must tackle under-age drinking and I would be in favour of introducing random breath tests for motorists, most of whom are not, of course, young adults. What is certain to continue is the contradiction in public policy between exercising more control (through electronic tagging or identity cards issued by publicans), and maximising profits (through extending licensing hours and the number of licensed premises).

Second, as problems become more complex, controversial and intractable, there is an understandable desire to reach out for a 'technological fix'. "There is a solution for every problem," wrote H L Mencken, "simple, easy and wrong." And yet we saw in the previous chapter how decision-makers tend to choose physical rather than social measures. Security systems of the most advanced kind have a part to play in a multiple strategy but they have been over-sold and their exclusive use constitutes a 'technological trap' for harassed administrators. We need a balanced, dispassionate and informed approach which can resist the temptation of thinking that technology will prove a panacea and which will insist on the evaluation of all policy initiatives. In the words of Anne Power (1989, p 232):

> ...it would be a grave mistake, based on the history of urban slums and the current crises in the Council housing sector, to place the emphasis on crime itself and on physical solutions while overlooking the much more deep-seated and elusive social and management problems of the most transient and least popular rented housing.

How confident can any of us feel that this "grave mistake" will be avoided?

Third, the easy equation of vandalism with young people, which is the standard reaction of the public and researchers alike and for which there is some statistical support, has made me increasingly uneasy because in another sphere I have seen how a national economic crisis in the late 1970s was transformed into a crisis of youth unemployment. That transformation captured the headlines because there were fears that fresh-faced sixteen year-olds with no future but the dole queue might cause trouble in the streets; but this concentration on the potential of the young unemployed for social unrest obscured the structural nature of the economic crisis and its unequal impact on various regions and certain sections of the community within all regions (see Chapter 5, point 4, for details). Bill Williamson (1990, p 275) has summed up the structure of feeling among young people in Britain at the beginning of the 1990s in this way:

All social change is achieved at some cost. What many young people have sensed is that the achievement of affluence...is something being bought at the cost of undermining their future prospects of jobs and the erosion of their effective rights as citizens.

No clearer demonstration of Williamson's argument could be made than the withdrawal of income support from 16 and 17 year olds by the Social Security Act of 1988. So all those under 18 who are unemployed are no longer officially recognised and, if not supported by their families, are not entitled to claim support.

Vandalism is not exclusively a crime committed by adolescents; indeed, French researchers (eg Moser, 1984, p 169) found that mature adults in both urban and rural areas were more frequently aggressive to malfunctioning public phones than either young or old persons. But when it comes to policy recommendations or educational initiatives, the criminal damage of adults is quietly forgotten. For instance, the TVS/British Telecom (1990, p 3) booklet on *Aspects of Vandalism* begins by arguing that criminal damage is "...not simply a young people's problem", but it immediately proceeds to introduce its two video films aimed exclusively at either 9-12 year-olds or 13-15 year-olds. Dan Cruickshank (1973, p 184) contrasts the way in which we all readily classify youngsters who rip up railway seats as vandals but "...developers who employ a demolition firm to bulldoze historically and socially irreplaceable structures are seen as business men, or as a democratically responsible authority, carrying out legitimate business". Such 'pinstripe' vandalism is not included in criminal statistics and may not even be recognised by many adults as vandalism. Readers will have their own favourite example of the destruction of historically irreplaceable buildings such as the demolition of the arch at Euston railway station, or of the medieval University College in Glasgow to make way for a railway goods station in 1860, or of Eldon Square in Newcastle to create a shopping mall in the 1960s.

Recently, the Home Secretary, Kenneth Baker (1991) emphasised that "...an alarming amount of crime is committed by young people - one third of all known offenders are under 17 and most of their crime is against property". By the same token, two thirds of all known offenders are 18 or over and so perhaps the concentration of efforts at prevention should be directed at the clear majority of offenders. **We are running the risk in Britain of making youth into a deviant category and treating all young people as though they were criminals or particularly prone to crime.** If we succeed in conveying that message rather than involving our young adults in responsible social participation, then they may very well live up to our expectations of them.

My final observations concern research into vandalism and I hope they will avoid the self-serving cliché of simply calling for more (but, of course, better) of the same. There is a direct parallel between the hit and run studies of vandalism carried out by most social scientists and the hit and run tactics of vandals and graffiti writers. Earlier chapters have shown that the research which has been carried out on vandalism, although prolific and varied, has not in the main been either cumulative or oriented towards policy. Differences in ideological stance have been reflected in subjective definitions of vandalism and contrasting methods of measurement. Comparative studies of vandalism in other European countries are vitiated for the same reasons. To enable researchers to build on each other's work **there needs to be agreement about how to define and measure vandalism**; Sturman (1978, p 18) has made useful suggestions which could form the basis of a new start and Cohen's typologies (explained in Chapter 3) are still useful.

The picture is far from gloomy. We have sufficient descriptive studies of the types and extent of vandalism (eg the writings of Stan Cohen and F J Gladstone which have been continually cited in this report), but what we need now are two different types of research. First, careful, independent evaluations of particular preventive measures which pay due attention to the processes of implementation, the amount of change which has been achieved, any unintended consequences which may result, and contradictions in policy which may become apparent (see Finch, 1988). Such critical assessments of the content, the quantity and the conditions surrounding the intervention would also benefit the development of theory; they also need to be longitudinal to give programmes like Neighbourhood Watch a chance to respond to the criticisms made earlier and to prove its worth.

Second, there is a place for ethnographic (or anthropological) studies of vandalism to explore systematically the negotiation of reality which takes place between the offender and the audience (head teachers, caretaker, or police) over the accounts given for criminal damage. Stan Cohen (1984, p 55) has begun to tease out the various possibilities; for example, when an actor offers a clear, political account ("I was protesting about the poll tax"), but the magistrate refuses to accept it ("This was nothing but senseless, wanton destruction"). Not only the political dimension of accounts could be studied, but also whether the actors accept responsibility or not for their behaviour and how the observers react to their claims; and how offenders assess the consequences of their actions in comparison with the views of residents and other members of the public.

Whatever the future direction of research, this country faces some crucial questions about our quality of life which is still much admired abroad. At the time of writing in March 1991, the Home Office has just released figures which show an increase in crimes notified to the police of 17.4% over last year, the largest yearly increase since 1974. The choices confronting us can be starkly put. We can follow the route already taken by the Americans with their black ghettoes and watch the steady growth in our inner-cities of an underclass with two (and sometimes even three) generations of the same family living off state benefits. Or we could continue much as we are in the hope of muddling through by increasing the powers available to the forces of law and order, by recruiting more police officers, and by turning our homes, schools and public buildings into mini-fortresses. **If theft and burglary continue to increase, the Englishman's home may indeed have to become a castle, electronically protected to fit a new age.**

There is another option available to us, but like the others it will be costly, exacting and controversial. It amounts to nothing less than a cultural change in the way we traditionally respond to crime and social problems generally; instead of the self-imposed injunction to 'act now, think later', we could plan a coherent and comprehensive programme of crime prevention, based on our understandings of the motives and meanings behind crime in particular and vandalism in particular. As a start, **we could begin to show through our actions that we value not only private possessions but also what we own collectively - for instance, parks, railway stations, and public buildings generally**. This recommendation, of course, would require a fundamental change in the attitude and legislative programme of government. There would also need to be sufficient resources to mount a multiple strategy to implement radical changes in housing, in the education, training and employment of young people and adults, in youth policy and in regional regeneration. **It is a tall order to call for cultural and political change of this magnitude but anything less will consign our cities and housing estates to a meaner, dirtier and more violent future.**

This report will, however, achieve its immediate objective if the voices of the powerless, struggling to communicate <u>through</u> vandalism and graffiti or struggling to cope with the effects <u>of</u> vandalism and graffiti are even faintly heard through these pages. Selosse (1984, p 48) accurately describes the response of young people when their words fail to penetrate the walls of adult indifference:

> *Since no one listens to them, adolescents exchange the audible register for the visible. In this way they leave their mark, create events and have apparent adventures. Young vandals refuse to remain dumb ie with no way of expressing themselves; they seek to communicate at all costs. Behind the marks left by their activity, they are the ones who will need to be looked at and, above all, listened to.*

APPENDIX

SOURCES OF PRACTICAL HELP

The following annotated list contains the details of the most useful resource materials which I came across during my long 'soak' in the literature. It is in no order of importance and is offered as a guide to those who may be new to the field and are looking for some starting points.

1. <u>Crime Concern</u> Crime Concern published in 1990 *Youth Crime Prevention: A Handbook of Good Practice* by Jim Findlay, Jon Bright and Kevin Gill. The aim is to prevent young people drifting into crime and to prevent them becoming its victims by involving them in imaginative activities which address their recreational, educational, training and employment needs. Grants of up to £200 are available to encourage young people's involvement in tackling the problem of vandalism. Submissions from England, Wales, Northern Ireland and the Channel Islands should be sent to: Jim Findlay, Crime Concern, David Murray John Building, Brunel Centre, Swindon, SN1 1LY (tel 0793-514596). Submissions from Scotland should go to: Kevin Gill, Crime Concern Scotland, 19 Elmbank Street, Glasgow, G2 4PB (tel 041-221-6130).

2. <u>Department of Education and Science</u> A number of practical publications are available from HMSO bookshops and those I would recommend include:

(i) DES (1983) *Vandalism in Schools and Colleges: Some Possible Ways of Reducing Damage,* Broadsheet 12, January. A useful four page summary of practical issues for LEAs and institutions.

(ii) DES (1987) *Crime Prevention in Schools: Practical Guidance,* Building Bulletin 67, London: HMSO contains guidelines on preventive measures which were based on nine months' research into vandalism, theft and fire in schools.

(iii) DES (1988) *Fire and the Design of Educational Buildings,* Building Bulletin 7, London: HMSO gives advice on the management and use of buildings in relation to fire safety.

(iv) DES (1989) *Crime Prevention in Schools: Specification, Installation and Maintenance of Intruder Alarm Systems*, Building Bulletin 69, London: HMSO describes the operation and application of various types of detectors and contains case studies of good installations in schools.

3. Educational Resources TVS in association with British Telecom has produced two video packs on *Aspects of Vandalism*, one aimed at 9-12 year-olds and the other at 13-15 year-olds. I have used the second video with 16 year-old Youth Trainees with considerable success; it certainly engaged them in exploring the nature and extent of vandalism in their own areas. The packs are available from TVS Education, TVS, Television Centre, Southampton, SO9 5HZ.

The Safe Neighbourhoods Unit (SNU) is producing a resource pack to help children gain an understanding of social and anti-social behaviour, crime, the law and how they can contribute to crime prevention. The pack is to be entitled *The Safer Primer* and could be used as the basis for work on citizenship, which is one of the cross-curricular themes proposed by the National Curriculum Council. For further details, contact SNU, 485/487 Bethnal Green Road, London, E2 9QH.

4. Graffiti Removal and Control A booklet with this title has been published in 1989 by CIRIA (Construction Industry Research and Information Association, 6 Storey's Gate, London, SW1P 3AU) and written by J Wallace and C Whitehead, Special Publication 71. The same booklet is available from DES, Architects and Building Branch, Elizabeth House, York Road, London, SE1 7PH. The booklet deals with graffiti removers, general procedures for removing graffiti and the costs involved.

5. The Council for Posterity/Institute for Social Inventions is running an Adopt-a-Planet project whereby pupils of all ages are encouraged to "adopt a little piece of the planet (adopt-a-stream, adopt-a-beach, adopt-a-street, adopt-a-park etc...)" in order to improve it and combat vandalism and graffiti. Further details from Nicholas Albery, 20 Heber Road, London, NW2 6AA.

6.The Design Council published in 1979 a useful guide (see Sykes, 1979) to the prevention of vandalism in housing estates, schools and children's playgrounds. It ends with a useful checklist of different types of damage and possible remedies or precautions that could be implemented.

BIBLIOGRAPHY

Allen, V L (1984) 'Toward an Understanding of the Hedonic Component of Vandalism'. In **Levy-Leboyer**, C (Ed), op cit, 77-89.

Arnstein, Sherry R (1969) 'Ladder of Citizen Participation', *Journal of the American Institute of Planners,* July, 216-224.

Ashton, David N, **Maguire**, Malcolm J and **Spilsbury**, Mark (1987) 'Labour Market Segmentation and the Structure of the Youth Labour Market'. In **Brown**, P and **Ashton**, D N (Eds) *Education, Unemployment and Labour Markets,* Lewes: Falmer Press.

Baker, Colin and **Waddon**, Alun (1989) 'Vandalism: understanding and prevention'. In **Reid**, Ken (Ed) *Helping Troubled Pupils in Secondary Schools,* Vol 2, Oxford: Blackwell.

Baker, Kenneth (1991) Speech to Neighbourhood Watch Co-ordinators Conference, 20 April, 1-7.

Baron, R M and **Fisher**, J D (1984) 'The Equity-Control Model of Vandalism: a refinement'. In **Levy-Leboyer**, C (Ed), op cit, 63-75.

Bottoms, A E (1974) Review of *Defensible Space* by **Newman**, O, *British Journal of Criminology,* 14, 2, 203-206.

Burrows, J (1980) 'Closed Circuit Television and Crime on the London Underground'. In **Clarke**, R V G and **Mayhew**, P (Eds) *Designing Out Crime,* Home Office Research Unit, London: HMSO.

Cairncross, Liz, **Clapham**, David and **Goodlad**, Robina (1989) *Tenant Participation in Housing Management,* London: TPAS/Institute of Housing.

Campbell, Anne (1987) *Girl Delinquents,* Oxford: Basil Blackwell.

Canter, D (1984) 'Vandalism: overview and prospect'. In **Levy-Leboyer**, C (Ed) op cit, 345-356.

Clarke, R V G (1977) 'Psychology and Crime', *Bulletin British Psychological Society,* 30, 280-283.

Clarke, R V G (Ed), (1978) *Tackling Vandalism,* Home Office Research Study No 47, London: HMSO.

Clarke, R V G (1984) 'Opportunity-Based Crime Rates', *British Journal of Criminology*, 24, 1, 74-83.

Clarke, R V G and **Mayhew**, P (Eds), (1980) *Designing Out Crime*, Home Office Research Unit, London: HMSO.

Cockburn, Cynthia (1987) *Two-Track Training: Sex Inequalities and the YTS*, Houndsmill, Basingstoke: Macmillan Education

Coffield, Frank, **Borrill**, Carol and **Marshall**, Sarah (1986) *Growing Up at the Margins: Young Adults in the North East*, Milton Keynes: Open University Press.

Coffield, Frank (1991a) 'From the Decade of the Enterprise Culture to the Decade of the TECs', *British Journal of Education and Work*, 4, 1, 59-78.

Coffield, Frank (1991b) 'A New National Plan for the Education, Training and Employment of 16-19 year-olds', Submission to the House of Commons Select Committee on Education, Science and the Arts.

Cohen, Stanley (1966) 'Vandalism: diagnosis of a disease', *New Education*, Vol 2, No 10, October, 10-15.

Cohen, Stanley (1968) 'The Politics of Vandalism', 'The Nature of Vandalism', 'Can It Be Controlled?', *New Society*, No 324, 12 December, 872-878.

Cohen, Stanley (1971a) Introduction to *Images of Deviance*, Harmondsworth: Penguin.

Cohen, Stanley (1971b) 'Directions for Research on Adolescent Group Violence and Vandalism', *British Journal of Criminology*, 11, 4, 319-40.

Cohen, Stanley (1973a) 'Property Destruction: motives and meanings'. In **Ward**, C (Ed) *Vandalism*, London: Architectural Press.

Cohen, Stanley (1973b) 'Campaigning against Vandalism'. In **Ward** C (Ed) *Vandalism*, London: Architectural Press.

Cohen, Stanley (1976) 'The Future of Vandalism', *Bulletin of Environmental Education*, No 60.

Cohen, Stanley (1984a) 'Sociological Approaches to Vandalism'. In **Levy-Leboyer**, C (Ed) op cit, 51-61.

Cohen, Stanley (1984b) 'The Public's Perception of Vandalism'. In **Levy-Leboyer**, C (Ed) op cit, 231-3.

Coleman, Alice (1985, revised 1990) *Utopia on Trial: Vision and Reality in Planned Housing,* London: Hilary Shipman.

Constable, H (1986) 'How to Succeed in Innovation - Stop Calling Inevitable Difficulties Failure', *Curriculum,* 7, 3, 162-169.

Cooper, Martha and **Chalfont**, Henry (1984) *Subway Art,* London: Thames and Hudson.

Cornish, D B and **Clarke**, R V G (1975) *Residential Treatment and its Effects on Delinquency,* Home Office Research Study No 32, London: HMSO.

Crime Concern Scotland (1991a) *Combating Vandalism in St Gregory's Secondary School,* Glasgow.

Crime Concern Scotland (1991b) *Combating Vandalism in Possilpark Secondary School,* Glasgow.

Croft, I J (1978) 'Foreword', in **Clarke**, R V G (Ed), *Tackling Vandalism,* Home Office Research Study No 47, London: HMSO.

Cruickshank, Dan (1973) 'Developers as Vandals'. In **Ward**, C (Ed) *Vandalism,* Architectural Press.

Dahrendorf, Ralph (1978) *The Underclass and the Future of Britain,* Windsor Castle: St George's House, 10th Annual Lecture.

Davies, Bernard (1986) *Threatening Youth: Towards a National Youth Policy,* Milton Keynes: Open University Press.

Dean, C and **Read**, S (1990) 'School Vandals' Parents Face Being Sued', *Times Educational Supplement,* 9 November, p 1.

Department of Education and Science (1983) *Vandalism in Schools and Colleges: Some Possible Ways of Reducing Damage,* Broadsheet 12, January.

Department of Education and Science (1987) *Crime Prevention in Schools: Practical Guidance,* Building Bulletin 67, London: HMSO.

Department of Education and Science (1988) *Fire and the Design of Educational Buildings,* Building Bulletin 7, London: HMSO.

Department of Education and Science (1989) *Crime Prevention in Schools: Specification, Installation and Maintenance of Intruder Alarm Systems,* Building Bulletin 69, London: HMSO.

Department of Education and Science (1990) *Security in Schools,* Paper by Architects and Building Branch, 7 June.

Department of the Environment (1977) *Housing Management and Design*, Lambeth Inner Area Study, London: Department of the Environment.

Dorn, Nick (1983) *Alcohol, Youth and the State*, London: Croom Helm.

Downes, David (1974) Review of *Vandalism* by Colin **Ward**, *British Journal of Criminology*, 14, 2, 203-206.

Ekblom, Paul (1988) 'The Case of Graffiti on London Underground Trains'. In TVS/British Telecom, *Combating Vandalism to Public Services*, London.

Ellerby, John (1966) 'Notes on Vandalism', Anarchy, 6, 3, 65-75.

Giller, Henri (1988) 'Vandalism and Public Payphones: summary of a pilot evaluation'. In TVS/British Telecom, *Combating Vandalism to Public Services*, London.

Gladstone, F J (1978) 'Vandalism among Adolescent Schoolboys'. In **Clarke**, R V G (Ed), (1978) *Tackling Vandalism*, Home Office Research Study, No 47, London: HMSO.

Gladstone, F J (1980) 'Co-ordinating Crime Prevention Efforts'. In **Clarke**, R V G and **Mayhew**, P (Eds) *Designing Out Crime*, Home Office Research Unit, London: HMSO.

Gofton, Les (1990) 'On the Town: Drink and the New Lawlessness', *Youth and Policy*, No 29, 33-39.

Goldman, N (1961) 'A Socio-Psychological Study of School Vandalism', *Crime and Delinquency*, 7, 221-230.

Graham, John (1988) *Schools, Disruptive Behaviour and Delinquency: A Review of Research*, Home Office Research Study 96, London: HMSO.

Graham, Marcus (1970) 'Vindicating a Villified Revolutionary', *Anarchy*, Vol 1, No 5, 8-12.

Greater London Council Police Committee (1984) *Vandalism in London*, County Hall, London.

Green, Andy (1988) 'Vandalism to Public Payphones'. In TVS/British Telecom, *Combating Vandalism to Public Services*, London.

Hall, P, **Land**, H, **Parker**, R and **Webb**, A (1975) *Change, Choice and Conflict in Social Policy*, London: Heinemann.

Hargreaves, David H (1982) *The Challenge for the Comprehensive School: Culture, Curriculum and Community*, London: Routledge and Kegan Paul.

Harrison, Paul (1985) *Inside the Inner City: Life under the Cutting Edge*, Harmondsworth: Penguin.

Harrison, Tony (1985) *V*, Newcastle: Bloodaxe Books.

Herbert, R L (1990) 'Arson and Vandalism in Schools: what can the educational psychologist do?', *Educational Psychology in Practice*, 6, 2, 65-70.

Heyne, Wilhelm (1987) *Spruche and Graffiti*, Munich: Wilhelm Heyne Verlag.

HMI (1991) *Standards in Education 1989-90*, Annual Report of HM Senior Chief Inspector of Schools, London: DES.

Hillier, Bill (1986) 'City of Alice's Dreams', *Architects Journal*, 9 July, 39-41

Hindelang, M J (1976) 'With a Little Help from their Friends: group participation in reported delinquent behaviour', *British Journal of Criminology*, 16, 2, 109-125.

Holloway, David (1989) *Untold Stories, Unseen Realms - The Report of the Exhibition of Graffiti Art*, London Union of Youth Clubs.

Home Office (1990) *Criminal Statistics, England and Wales 1989*, London: HMSO, Cm 1322.

Hope, Tim (1984) 'Preventing Vandalism: the experience of an action research project'. In **Levy-Leboyer**, C (Ed), op cit, 335-343.

Hough, J M et al (1980) 'Introduction'. In **Clarke**, R V G and **Mayhew**, P (Eds) *Designing Out Crime*, Home Office Research Unit, London: HMSO.

Hurd, Douglas (1988) Address to Conference, *Combating Vandalism to Public Services*, London, 28 June: TVS/British Telecom.

Jacobs, Jane (1961) *The Death and Life of Great American Cities*, New York: Vintage.

Jones, Trevor (1988) 'Crime Prevention and Local Authorities: Islington Council, a case study'. In TVS/British Telecom, op cit, 22-24.

King, Michael (1988) *The French Experience: How to make Social Crime Prevention Work*, London: NACRO.

Leather, Alan and **Matthews**, Antony (1973) 'What the Architect Can Do: a series of design studies'. In **Ward**, C (Ed) *Vandalism*, London: Architectural Press.

Lee, David, **Marsden**, Dennis, **Rickman**, Penny and **Duncombe**, Jean (1990) *Scheming for Youth: A Study of YTS in the Enterprise Culture*, Milton Keynes: Open University Press.

Levy-Leboyer, Claude (1984) (Ed) *Vandalism: Behaviour and Motivations*, Amsterdam: Elsevier Science.

Lindley, Robert (1987) (Ed) *Review of the Economy and Employment, 1987*, University of Warwick: Institute for Employment Research.

McGregor, Ian (1988) 'Vandalism on Britain's Railways'. In TVS/British Telecom, *Combating Vandalism to Public Services*, London.

Mailer, Norman (1974) *The Faith of Graffiti*, New York: Praeger/Alskog.

Mair, George and **Nee**, Claire (1990) *Electronic Monitoring: The Trials and Their Results*, Home Office Research Study No 120, London: HMSO.

Marcus, C L (1984) 'British Telecom Experience in Payphone Management'. In **Levy-Leboyer**, C (Ed), op cit, 311-318.

Markus, Thomas A (1988) 'Rehumanizing the Dehumanized'. In **Teymur**, N, **Markus**, T A and **Woolley**, T, (Eds) *Rehumanizing Housing*, London: Butterworths, 1-15.

Marsh, P, **Rosser**, E and **Harré**, R (1978) *The Rules of Disorder*, London: Routledge and Kegan Paul.

Martin, J M (1961) *Juvenile Vandalism*, Springfield, Illinois: Charles C Thomas.

Mawby, R I (1977) 'Kiosk Vandalism: a Sheffield study', *British Journal of Criminology*, 17, 1, 30-46.

May, Pete (1989) 'Understanding the Graffiti Sub-culture', *Crime Prevention News*, Summer, 7-9.

Mayhew, P (1979) 'Defensible Space: the current status of a crime prevention theory', *The Howard Journal of Penology and Crime Prevention*, 18, 150-159.

Mayhew, P, **Clarke**, R V G and **Hough**, J M (1980a) 'Steering Column Locks and Car Theft'. In **Clarke**, R V G and **Mayhew**, P (Eds) *Designing Out Crime*, Home Office Research Unit, London: HMSO.

Mayhew, P et al (1980b) 'Natural Surveillance and Vandalism to Telephone Kiosks'. In **Clarke**, R V G and **Mayhew**, P (Eds) *Designing Out Crime*, Home Office Research Unit, London: HMSO.

Mayhew, P et al (1989) *The 1988 British Crime Survey*, Home Office Research Study No 111, London: HMSO.

Mays, J B (1954) *Growing up in the City*, Liverpool: University Press.

Morgan, Elaine (1978) *Falling Apart: The Rise and Decline of Urban Civilization*, London: Abacus: Sphere Books.

Moser, G (1984) 'Everyday Vandalism: public telephones'. In **Levy-Leboyer**, C (Ed) op cit, 167-174.

Moser, G, Girault, N and **Levy-Leboyer**, C (1984) 'The Evaluation of Acts of Vandalism'. In **Levy-Leboyer**, C (Ed) op cit, 247-255.

NACRO (1988) *Growing Up on Housing Estates*, London.

Naidoo, Jennie (1986) 'Limits to Individualism'. In **Rodmell**, Sue and **Watt**, Alison (Eds) *The Politics of Health Education: Raising the Issues*, London: Routledge and Kegan Paul.

Newman, O (1972) *Defensible Space: Crime Prevention Through Urban Design*, New York: Macmillan.

Newman, O (1976) *Design Guidelines for Creating Defensible Space*, National Institute of Law Enforcement and Criminal Justice, Washington, DC: Government Printing Office.

Newman, O (1980) *Community of Interest*, New York: Anchor Press/ Doubleday.

Nisbet, John (1975) 'Innovation - Bandwaggon or Hearse?' In **Harris**, Alan, **Lawn**, Martin and **Prescott**, William (Eds) *Curriculum Innovation*, London: Croom Helm.

Norris, Steve (1988) 'Combating Vandalism to Public Services'. In TVS/ British Telecom, op cit, 32.

North East Regional Schools Security Group (1990) *Security in Schools: A Management Guide*, Newcastle.

Noschis, K (1984) 'Countries without Vandalism?' In **Levy-Leboyer**, C (Ed) op cit, 91-101.

Oxford, Sir Kenneth (1988) Address to Conference, *Combating Vandalism to Public Services*, London, 28 June: TVS/British Telecom.

Pahl, Raymond (1984) *Divisions of Labour*, Oxford: Basil Blackwell.

Pollard, Dennis (1988) *Attitudes to Vandalism: A Survey of 13-16 year-olds*, Northumbria Police.

Power, Anne (1989) 'Housing, Community and Crime'. In **Downes**, D (Ed) *Crime in the City*, Basingstoke: Macmillan.

Pullen, David (1973) 'Community Involvement'. In **Ward**, C (Ed) *Vandalism,* London: Architectural Press.

Ravetz, Alison (1988) 'Malaise, Design and History: scholarship and experience on trial'. In **Teymur**, M, **Markus**, T and **Woolley**, T (Eds) *Rehumanizing Housing,* London: Butterworths, 154-165.

Rees, Nigel (1982) *Graffiti 4,* London: Unwin.

Riley, D and **Shaw**, M (1985) *Parental Supervision and Juvenile Delinquency,* Home Office Research Study No 83, London: HMSO.

Riley, D (1980) 'An Evaluation of a Campaign to Reduce Vandalism'. In **Clarke**, R V G and **Mayhew**, P (Eds) *Designing Out Crime,* Home Office Research Unit, London: HMSO.

Roberts, Sharon (1990) *Seminar Report on Graffiti Art,* London Union of Youth Clubs.

Rose, David (1991) 'Crime: the facts', *Observer Magazine,* 17 February, 22-33.

Rosenbaum, Dennis P (1987) 'The Theory and Research Behind Neighbourhood Watch: is it a sound fear and crime reduction strategy?', *Crime and Delinquency,* 33, 1, 103-134.

Rutter, M, **Maughan**, B, **Mortimore**, P and **Ouston**, J (1979) *Fifteen Thousand Hours,* Open Books.

Rutter, Michael and **Giller**, Henri (1983) *Juvenile Delinquency: Trends and Perspectives,* Harmondsworth: Penguin.

Scarman, The Lord (1987) *The Brixton Disorders 10-12 April 1987,* London: HMSO, Cm 8427.

Schama, Simon (1989) *Citizens: A Chronicle of the French Revolution,* London: Viking.

Selosse, J (1984) 'Vandalism: speech acts'. In **Levy-Leboyer**, C (Ed) op cit, 39-49.

Sloan-Howitt, M and **Kelling**, G L (1990) 'Subway Graffiti in New York City: 'Getting Up' vs 'Meaning It and Cleaning It'', *Security Journal,* 1, 3, 131-136.

Sperandio (1984), 'Vandalism as a Fact of Life in Society'. In **Levy-Leboyer**, C (Ed) op cit, 105-107.

Sturman, A (1978) 'Measuring Vandalism in a City Suburb'. In **Clarke**, R V G (Ed) *Tackling Vandalism*, Home Office Research Study No 47, London: HMSO.

Sturman, A (1980) 'Damage on Buses: the effects of supervision'. In **Clarke**, R V G and **Mayhew**, P (Eds) *Designing Out Crime*, Home Office Research Unit, London: HMSO.

Sykes, Jane (Ed) (1979) *Designing Against Vandalism*, London: Design Council/Heinemann.

Taylor, Ian (1971) 'Social Work and the Soccer Hooligan', *Social Work Today*, 2, 12, 23 September, 25-27.

Taylor, Ian and **Walton**, Paul (1973) 'Hey, Mister, This Is What We Really Do...'. In **Ward**, C (Ed) *Vandalism*, London: Architectural Press.

Taylor, Laurie (1973) 'The Meaning of the Environment'. In **Ward**, C (Ed) *Vandalism*, London: Architectural Press.

Taylor, Laurie and **Walton**, Paul (1971) 'Industrial Sabotage: Motives and Meanings'. In **Cohen**, S (Ed) *Images of Deviance*, Harmondsworth: Penguin.

Tuck, Mary (1989) *Drinking and Disorder: A Study of Non-Metropolitan Violence*, Home Office Research Study No 108, London: HMSO.

Tutt, Norman (1988) 'Preventing Vandalism - Action for Local Authorities'. In TVS/British Telecom, op cit, 25-26.

TVS/British Telecom (1988) *Combating Vandalism to Public Services: A Programme for the 1990s*, London: Report of Conference, 28 June.

TVS/British Telecom (1990) *Aspects of Vandalism: An Educational Video Resource*, Southampton: TVS Education.

Van Dijk, B, **Van Soomeren**, and **Walop**, M (1984) 'Vandalism in Amsterdam'. In **Levy-Leboyer**, C (Ed) op cit, 319-334.

Van Vliet, W (1984) 'Vandalism: an assessment and agenda'. In **Levy-Leboyer**, C (Ed) op cit, 14-36.

Wade, A L (1967) 'Social Processes in the Act of Juvenile Vandalism'. In **Clinard**, M B and **Quinney**, R (Eds) *Criminal Behaviour Systems*, New York: Holt, Rhinehard and Winston.

Ward, Colin (1973) (Ed) *Vandalism*, London: Architectural Press.

Ward, Colin (1990) Discussion Paper on Vandalism and Graffiti, Calouste Gulbenkian Foundation, London, 18 June, 1-10.

Washington Development Corporation (1972) *Vandalism: A Study of Washington New Town*, Washington.

Wawrzynski, J K (1984) 'Vandalism in Residential Areas in England: Oldham case study'. In **Levy-Leboyer**, C (Ed) op cit, 283-294.

West, D J (1969) *Present Conduct and Future Delinquency*, London: Heinemann.

West, D J (1973a) *Who Becomes Delinquent?*, London: Heinemann.

West, D J (1973b) 'Are Delinquents Different?', *New Society*, 22 November, 466-8.

West, D J and **Farrington**, D P, (1977) *The Delinquent Way of Life*, London: Heinemann.

Williamson, Bill (1990) *The Temper of the Times: British Society Since World War II*, Oxford: Basil Blackwell.

Wilson, Paul R (1990) 'Reduction of Telephone Vandalism: An Australian Case Study', *Security Journal*, 1, 3, 149-154.

Wilson, S (1980) 'Vandalism and 'Defensible Space' on London Housing Estates'. In **Clarke**, R V G and **Mayhew**, P (Eds) *Designing Out Crime*, Home Office Research Unit, London: HMSO.

Zimbardo, Philip G (1973) 'A Field Experiment in Auto Shaping'. In **Ward**, C (Ed) *Vandalism*, London: Architectural Press.

Zwier, G and **Vaughan**, G M (1984) 'Three Ideological Orientations in School Vandalism Research', *Review of Educational Research*, 54, 2, 263-292.